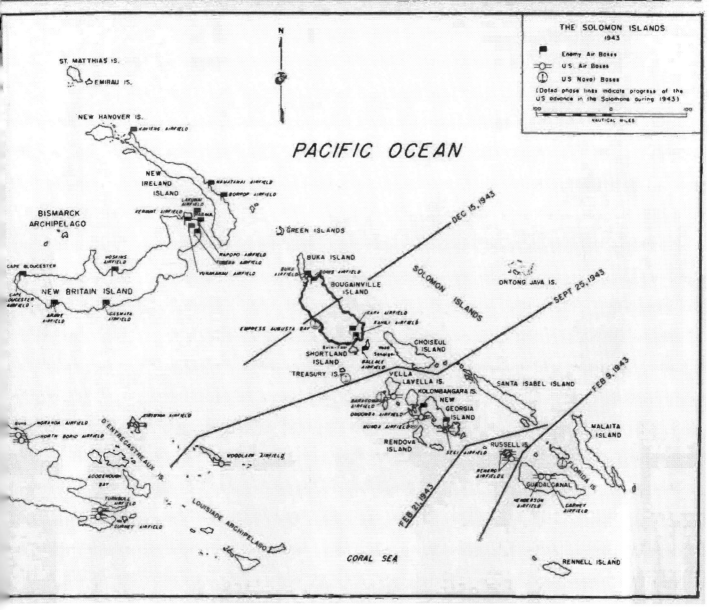

PACIFIC OCEAN

THE SOLOMON ISLANDS
1943

▐ Enemy Air Bases
⌀ U.S. Air Bases
① US Naval Bases

(Dotted phase lines indicate progress of the
US advance in the Solomons during 1943)

100   0   100
NAUTICAL MILES

Time of the Aces:
Marine Pilots in the Solomons

by Commander Peter B. Mersky, U.S. Naval Reserve

The morale of the men of the 1st Marine Division on Guadalcanal soared dramatically in the late afternoon of 20 August 1942. That was when 19 Grumann F4F Wildcats of Captain John L. Smith's Marine Fighter Squadron (VMF) 223 and 12 Douglas Dauntless SBDs of Major Richard C. Mangrum's Marine Scout-Bomber Squadron (VMSB) 232 landed on yet-uncompleted Henderson Field. Ever since the assault landing on Guadalcanal on 7 August, and subject to unchallenged Japanese air raids from that time, the ground troops wondered, "Where are our planes?" Like so many other soldiers in so many other campaigns, they had little knowledge of the progress of the war elsewhere in the Pacific.

From the very beginning of World War II, with the Japanese attack on Wake Island, Marine aircraft, pilots, and crews became immediately and personally involved in the fighting. On Wake, Marine Wildcat pilots of VMF-211 gave a good account of themselves, even after the number of the squadron's flyable planes was reduced to four, and when those planes were damaged beyond repair, all aviation personnel became riflemen. And in the Battle of Midway, Marine pilots for the first time at first hand apprehended the nature of the war in the air as they flew against combat-experienced Japanese aircrews. But by the time of the landings on Guadalcanal and when the war was nearly a year old, only a relatively small number of Marine pilots had seen combat. A few had shot down several Japanese aircraft, although none had scored a fifth kill which would entitle him to be designated an ace. The leading Marine scorer at Midway was Captain Marion Carl, who had downed two Mitsubishi Type "O" Carrier Fighters. The Americans would later call them "Zeros" or "Zekes" and would shoot them down regularly despite the early reputation they received for being a highly maneuverable and deadly adversary in the air. Before he left the Pacific, Captain Carl would add considerably to his score, as would some of the other fighter pilots who landed on Guadalcanal with him on the 20th.

Guadalcanal: The Beginning of the Long Road Back

Marine Aircraft Group (MAG) 23, the initial air unit participating in the Guadalcanal operation, was assigned the mission of supporting the ground operations of the 1st Marine Division as well the air defense of the island once the landing had been made. MAG-23 included VMF-223 and -224, and VMSB-231 and -232. The fighter squadrons flew the F4F-4, the Grumann Wildcat with folding wings and six wing-mounted .50-caliber machine guns. The two VMSBs flew the Douglas SBD-3 Dauntless dive-bomber. Another fighter squadron, VMF-212, under Major Harold W. Bauer, was on the island of Efate in the New Hebrides, while MAG-23 headquarters had yet to sail from Hawaii by the time Marines hit the beaches on 7 August 1942. The first contingent of MAG-23—VMF-223 and VMSB-232—left Hawaii on board the escort carrier USS *Long Island* (CVE 1). On 20 August, 200 miles from Guadalcanal, the two squadrons launched toward their new home. VMF-224 (Captain Robert E. Galer) and VMSB-231 (Major Leo R. Smith) followed in the aircraft transports USS *Kitty*

The Douglas SBD Dauntless divebomber fought in nearly every theater, flying with the U.S. Navy and Marine Corps, as well as the U.S. Army (as the A-24 Banshee). The SBD made its reputation in the Pacific, especially at Midway and Guadalcanal.

Author's Collection

Department of Defense Photo (USMC) 26044

Capt Henry T. Elrod, a Wildcat pilot with VMF-211, earned what is chronologically the first Marine Corps—but not the first actually awarded—Medal of Honor for World War II. His exploits during the defense of Wake Island were not known until after the war. After his squadron's aircraft were all destroyed, Capt Elrod fought on the ground and was finally killed by a Japanese rifleman.

Hawk (APV 1) and USS *Hammondsport* (APV 2), and flew on to the island on 30 August. While en route toward the launch point for Guadalcanal, Captain Smith wisely decided to trade eight of his less experienced junior pilots for eight pilots of VMF-212 who had more flight time and training in the F4F than had Smith's fledglings.

The newly arrived squadrons barely had time to get settled before they were in heavy action. Early on the 21st, the Japanese sent a 900-man force to attack Henderson Field, named after Major Lofton R. Henderson, a dive-bomber pilot killed at Midway. Around mid-day, Captain Smith was leading a four-plane patrol north of Savo Island heading toward the Russell Islands with Second Lieutenants Noyes McLennan and Charles H. Kendrick, and Technical Sergeant John Lindley. The two lieutenants had 16 days of operational flight training in F4Fs, and Lindley had been through ACTG,

the Aircraft Carrier Training Group, which, as part of its training syllabus, gave tyro pilots indoctrination into fighter tactics.

Beyond Savo, six Zeros came straight at them from the north, with an altitude advantage of 500 feet. Smith recognized the Zeros immediately, although neither he nor any of the other three pilots had ever seen one before. He turned his flight toward them and the Zeros headed toward the F4Fs.

It was hard to say just what happened next except that the Zero Smith was shooting at pulled up and he shot fairly well into the belly of the enemy plane as it went by, only to find that now he had two Zeros on his tail. Captain Smith dove toward Henderson Field and the Japs broke away.

Minutes later, the Zero Captain Smith shot became VMF-223's first kill when it crashed into the water just off Savo Island. Smith's plane had some bullet holes but was flying alright. Two F4Fs joined on him. They looked back and it appeared that the Zeros were in a dogfight near Savo. The Marines thought they were ganging up on Sergeant Lindley so they went back to help him, but found that there was no F4F, just five Zeros acting like they were fighting.

The three Marines then got into another dogfight and the Zeros shot them up some more. Lindley and Kendrick got back to Henderson and made dead-stick landings. Lindley was burned and blinded by hot oil when his oil tank was shattered and landed wheels up. Kendrick's oil line was shot away and he crash-landed. His airplane never flew again. It took eight days before Smith's plane was patched up enough to fly once again. Repairs on the fourth plane required 10 days. Only 15 of the 19 F4Fs were flyable after their first day of action from Henderson Field.

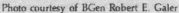

Members of VMF-224 pose by one of their fighters on Guadalcanal in mid-September 1942. Rear row, left to right: 2dLt George L. Hollowell, SSgt Clifford D. Garrabrant, 2dLt Robert A Jefferies, Jr., 2dLt Allan M. Johnson, 2dLt Matthew H. Kennedy, 2dLt Charles H. Kunz, 2dLt Dean S. Hartley, Jr., MG William R. Fuller. Front row: 2dLt Robert M. D'Arcy, Capt Stanley S. Nicolay, Maj John F. Dobbin, Maj Robert E. Galer, Maj Kirk Armistead, Capt Dale D. Irwin, 2dLt Howard L. Walter, 2dLt Gordon E. Thompson. All in this picture are pilots except MG Fuller, who was the Engineering Officer. Lt Thompson was reported missing in action on 31 August 1942.
Photo courtesy of BGen Robert E. Galer

'CUB One' at Guadalcanal

On 8 August 1942, U.S. Marines captured a nearly completed enemy airstrip on Guadalcanal, which would prove critical to the success of the island campaign. It was essential that the airstrip become operational as quickly as possible, not only to contest enemy aircraft in the skies over Guadalcanal, but also to ensure that badly needed supplies could be flown in and wounded Marines flown out. As it turned out, Henderson Field also proved to be a safe haven for Navy planes whose carriers had been sunk or badly damaged.

A Marine fighter squadron (VMF-223) and a Marine dive bomber squadron (VMSB-232) were expected to arrive on Guadalcanal around 16 August. Unfortunately, Marine aviation ground crews scheduled to accompany the two squadrons to Guadalcanal were still in Hawaii, and would not arrive on the island for nearly two weeks. Aircraft ground crews were urgently needed to service the two Marine squadrons upon their arrival.

The nearest aircraft ground crews to Guadalcanal were not Marines, but 450 Navy personnel of a unit known as CUB One, an advanced base unit consisting of the personnel and material necessary for the establishment of a medium-sized advanced fuel and supply base. CUB One had only recently arrived at Espiritu Santo in the New Hebrides.

On 13 August, Admiral John S. McCain ordered Marine Major Charles H. "Fog" Hayes, executive officer of Marine Observation Squadron 251, to proceed to Guadalcanal with 120 men of CUB One to assist Marine engineers in completing the airfield (recently named Henderson Field in honor of a Marine pilot killed in the Battle of Midway), and to serve as ground crews for the Marine fighters and dive bombers scheduled to arrive within a few days. Navy Ensign George W. Polk was in command of the 120-man unit, and was briefed by Major Hayes concerning the unit's critical mission. (After the war, Polk became a noted newsman for the Columbia Broadcasting System, and was murdered by terrorists during the Greek Civil War. A prestigious journalism award was established and named in his honor).

Utilizing four destroyer transports of World War I vintage, the 120-man contingent from CUB One departed Espiritu Santo on the evening of 13 August. The total supply carried northward by the four transports included 400 drums of aviation gasoline, 32 drums of lubricant, 282 bombs (100 to 500 pounders), belted ammunition, a variety of tools, and critically needed spare parts.

The echelon arrived at Guadalcanal on the evening of 15 August, unloaded its passengers and supplies, and began assisting Marine engineers the following morning on increasing the length of Henderson Field. In spite of daily raids by Japanese aircraft, the arduous work continued, and on 19 August, the airstrip was completed. CUB One personnel also installed and manned an air-raid warning system in the famous "Pagoda," the Japanese-built control tower.

On 20 August, 19 planes of VMF-223 and 12 dive bombers of VMSB-232 were launched from the escort carrier *Long Island* and arrived safely at Henderson Field. The Marine pilots were quickly put into action over the skies of Guadalcanal in combat operations against enemy aircraft.

The men of CUB One performed heroics in servicing the newly arrived Marine fighters and bombers. Few tools existed or had yet arrived to perform many of the aircraft servicing jobs to which CUB One was assigned. It was necessary to fuel the Marine aircraft from 55-gallon drums of gasoline. As there were no fuel pumps on the island, the drums had to be man-handled and tipped into the wing tanks of the SBDs and the fuselage tanks of the F4F fighters. To do this, CUB One personnel stood precariously on the slippery wings of the aircraft and sloshed the gasoline from the heavy drums into the aircraft's gas tanks. The men used a make-shift funnel made from palm-log lumber.

Bomb carts or hoists were also at a premium during the early days of the Guadalcanal campaign, so aircraft bombs had to be raised by hand to the SBD drop brackets, as the exhausted, straining men wallowed in the mud beneath the airplanes.

No automatic belting machines were available at this time as well, so that the .50-caliber ammunition for the four guns on each fighter had to be hand-belted one round at a time by the men of CUB One. The gunners on the dive bombers loaded their ammunition by the same laborious method.

The dedicated personnel of CUB One performed these feats for 12 days before Marine squadron ground crews arrived with the proper equipment to service the aircraft. The crucial support provided by CUB One was instrumental to the success of the "Cactus Air Force" on Guadalcanal.

Like their Marine counterparts, the personnel of CUB One suffered from malaria, dengue fever, sleepless nights, and the ever-present shortage of food, clothing, and supplies. They would remain on Guadalcanal, performing their duties in an exemplary manner, until relieved on 5 February 1943. CUB One richly earned the Presidential Unit Citation awarded to the unit for its gallant participation in the Guadalcanal campaign.

—Arvil L. Jones with Robert V. Aquilina

Allied air operations in the Solomons were controlled from the "Pagoda," built by the Japanese and rehabilitated by the men of CUB One.

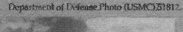
Department of Defense Photo (USMC) 51812.

Photo courtesy of Capt Stanley S. Nicolay

Three personalities of the Cactus Air Force pose after receiving the Navy Cross from Adm Nimitz on 30 September 1942. From left: Maj John L. Smith, Maj Robert E. Galer, and Capt Marion E. Carl.

Marion Carl, now assigned to VMF-223, shot down three Japanese aircraft on 24 August to become the Marine Corps' first ace. Carl added two more kills on the 26th. The young fighter pilot found himself in competition with his squadron commander, as John Smith also began accumulating kills with regularity.

The 30th was a busy day for the Marine fighters on Guadalcanal. The previous day's action saw eight Japanese aircraft shot down. However, by now, six of VMF-223's original complement of 19 Wildcats had also been destroyed or put out of action. The combat had been fast and furious since Smith and his squadron had arrived only nine days before. His young pilots were learning, but at a price.

One of the squadrons that shared Henderson Field with the Marines was the 67th Fighter Squadron, a somewhat orphaned group of Army Air Corps pilots, who had arrived on 22 August, led by Captain Dale Brannon, and their P-400 Airacobras, an export version of the Bell P-39. Despite its racy looks, the Airacobra found it difficult to get above 15,000 feet, where much of the aerial combat was taking place.

The 67th had had a miserable time of it so far because of their plane's poor performance, and morale was low. The pilots were beginning to question their value to the overall effort, and their commander, desperate for any measure of success to share with his men, asked Captain Smith if he and his squadron could accompany the Marines on their next scramble.

Smith agreed and on 30 August, the Marine and Army fighters—eight F4Fs and seven P-400s—launched for a lengthy combat air patrol.

The fighters rendezvoused north of Henderson, maintaining 15,000 feet because of the P-400s' lack of oxygen. Coastwatchers had identified a large formation of Japanese bombers heading toward Henderson but had lost sight of their quarry in the rapidly building wall of thunderclouds approaching the island. The defenders orbited for 40 minutes, watching for the enemy bombers and their escorts.

Suddenly, Captain Smith saw the seven Army fighters dive toward the water, in hot pursuit of Zeros that had emerged from the clouds. The highly maneuverable Zeros quickly turned the tables on the P-400s, however. As the Japanese fighters concentrated on the hapless Bells, the Marine Wildcats lined up behind the Zeros and quickly shot down four of the dark green Mitsubishis. The effect of the F4Fs' heavy machine guns was devastating.

Making a second run, Captain Smith found himself going head-to-head with a Zero, its pilot just as de-

A profile of Bell P-39 Airacobra by Larry Lapadura. "Short Stroke" operated from Henderson Field on Guadalcanal from late 1942 to early 1943. The aircraft's deceptively streamlined shape belied a mediocre performance, especially above 15,000 feet. However, the aircraft was well armed and used with success as a ground strafer.

Author's Collection

Department of Defense Photo (USMC) 11984

Maj John L. Smith poses in a Wildcat after returning to the States. A tough, capable combat leader, Smith received the Medal of Honor for his service at Guadalcanal.

Photo courtesy of Capt Stanley S. Nicolay

1stLt Stanley S. Nicolay beside a Wildcat, probably just before deploying to the Pacific in 1942. He eventually shot down three Betty bombers at Guadalcanal. Note the narrow track of the Wildcat's main landing gear.

termined as his Marine opponent. Smith's guns finally blew the Zero up just before a collision or before one of the two fighter pilots would have had to turn away. By the end of the engagement, John Smith had shot down two more Zeros for a total of four kills. With nine kills, Smith was the leading Marine Corps ace at the time. Fourteen Japanese fighters—the bombers they were escorting had turned back—had been shot down by the Marine and Army pilots, although four of the P-400s were also destroyed. Two of the pilots returned to Guadalcanal; two did not.

The Marine fighter contingent at Guadalcanal was now down to five operational aircraft; it needed reinforcement immediately. Help was on the way, however, for VMF-224 arrived in the afternoon of the 30th, after John Smith and his tired, but elated squadron returned from their frantic encounter with the Japanese fighter force. For their first few missions, VMF-224's pilots accompanied the now-veteran Rainbow Squadron pilots of VMF-223.*

---

* When it was first established on 1 May 1942, VMF-223 was called the "Rainbow" Squadron. In May 1943, it changed its nickname to the more Marine-like "Bulldogs."

Captain Galer's VMF-224 had no time to acclimate to its new base. (The day after its arrival, it was in action.) The squadron landed on the 30th in the midst of an alert, and was quickly directed to its parking areas on the field.

The next two weeks saw several of the Marine aviators bail out of their Wildcats after tangling with the enemy Zeros. On 31 August, First Lieutenant Stanley S. Nicolay of VMF-224 was on a flight with Second Lieutenant Richard R. Amerine, Second Lieutenant Charles E. Bryans, and Captain John F. Dobbin, the squadron executive officer. It was VMF-224's first combat mission since its arrival the day before. As the Marines struggled past 18,000 feet on their way up to 20,000, Lieutenant Nicolay noticed two of the wingmen lagging farther and farther back.

He called Amerine and Bryans but got no response. He then called Dobbin and said he wanted to drop back to check on the wayward Wildcats. "It's too late to break up

the formation," Dobbin wisely said. "There's nothing we can do." Nicolay closed up on Dobbin and they continued on.

The two young aviators had problems with their primitive oxygen systems and lacking sufficient oxygen, they possibly had even passed out in the thin air. Nicolay recalled,

> We never saw Bryans again. It was so senseless. I remember thinking that after all their training and effort, neither one of them ever fired a shot in anger. They had no chance. The oxygen system was just a tiny, white triangular mask that fitted over the nose and mouth. You turned on the bottle, and that was it. No pressure system, nothing.

Apparently, the two Marine pilots had been jumped by roving Zeros. Bryans was thought to be killed almost immediately, while Amerine was able to bail out. He parachuted to the relative safety of the jungle, and as he attempted to return to Henderson Field, he encountered several Japanese patrols on the way back, killing four enemy soldiers before returning to the Marine lines.

Marion Carl, who had 11 kills, had his own escape-and-evasion experience after he and his wingman, Lieutenant Clayton M. Canfield, were shot down on 9 September. Carl bailed out of his burning Wildcat and landed in the water where a friendly native scooped him up and hid him from the roving Japanese patrols. (Canfield had been quickly rescued by an American destroyer.)

The native took the ace to a native doctor who spoke English. The doctor gave Carl a small boat with an old motor which needed some work before it functioned properly. With the Japanese army all around, it was important that the American pilot get out as soon as he could.

Finally, he and the doctor arrived offshore of Marine positions on Guadalcanal. Dennis Byrd recalled Carl's return on the afternoon of 14 September:

A small motor launch operated by a very black native with a huge head of frizzled hair pulled up to the Navy jetty at Kukum. The tall white man tending the boat's wheezing engine was VMF-223's Captain Marion Carl. He had been listed as missing in action since September 9th and was presumed dead....Carl reported that on the day he disappeared, he'd shot down two more Jap bombers. Captain Carl's score was now 12 and Major Smith's, 14.

Now-Major Galer scored his squadron's first kills when he shot down two Zeros during a noontime raid of 26 bombers and eight Zero escorts over Henderson on 5 September. VMF-224 went up to intercept them, and the squadron commander knocked down a bomber

National Archives photo 208-PU-14X-1 PNT

A rare photo of an exuberant LtCol Bauer as he demonstrates his technique to two ground crewmen. Intensely competitive, and known as "the Coach," Bauer was one of several Marine Corps aviators who received the Medal of Honor, albeit posthumously, at Guadalcanal.

and a fighter, after which he was shot down by a Zero that tacked onto him from behind and riddled his Wildcat. Recalling the action in a wartime press release, Galer said:

I knew I'd be forced to land, but that Zero getting me dead to rights made me sore. I headed into a cloud, and instead of coming out below it as he expected, I came out on top and let him have it....

Then we both fell, but he was in flames and done for. I made a forced landing in a field, and before my wheels could stop rolling, Major Rivers J. Morrell and Lieutenant Pond of VMF-223, both forced their ships on the same deck—all within three minutes of each other!

Two days after his forced landing, Major Galer had to ditch his aircraft once more after another round with the Japanese. His flight was returning from a mission when it ran into a group of enemy

bombers. He related that:

One of them fell to my guns, and pulling out of the dive, I took after a Zero. But I didn't pull around fast enough, and his guns knocked out my engine, setting it on fire. We were at about 5,000 feet, but I feared the swirling mass of Japs more than the fire . . . so I laid over on my back and dove headlong for some clouds below me. Coming through the clouds, I didn't see any more Japs, and leveled off at 2,000 feet. I changed my angle of flight and grade of descent so I'd land as near as possible to shore. I set down in the drink some 200 or 300 yards from shore and swam in, unhurt.*

*This was not the first time Galer had a watery end to a flight. As a first lieutenant with VMF-2 in 1940, he had to ride his Grumman F3F biplane fighter in while approaching the carrier *Saratoga* (CV3). The Grumman sank and stayed on the bottom off San Diego for 40 years. It was discovered by a Navy exploration team and raised, somewhat the worse for wear. Retired Brigadier General Robert Galer was at the dock when his old mount found dry land once more.

The Aircraft in the Conflict

The U.S. Navy and Marine Corps were definitely at a disadvantage when America entered World War II in December 1941. Besides other areas, their frontline aircraft were well behind world standards.

The Japanese did not suffer similarly, however, for they were busy building up their arsenal as they sought sources of raw materials they needed and were prepared to go to war to acquire. Besides possessing what was the finest aerial torpedo in the world—the Long Lance—they had the aircraft to deliver it. And they had fighters to protect the bombers. Although the world initially refused to believe how good Japanese aircraft and their pilots were, it wasn't long after the attack on Pearl Harbor that reality seeped in.

In many respects, the U.S. Army Air Force—it had been the U.S. Army Air Corps until 20 June 1941—and the Navy and Marine Corps had the same problems in the first two years of the war. The Army's top fighters were the Bell P-39 Airacobra and the Curtiss P-40B/E Tomahawk/Kittyhawk. The Navy and Marine Corps' two frontline fighters were the Brewster F2A-3 Buffalo and the Grumman F4F-3/4 Wildcat during 1942.

Of these single-seaters, only the Army's P-40 and the Navy's F4F achieved any measure of success against the Japanese in 1942. The P-40's main attributes were its diving speed, which let it disengage from a fight, and its ability to absorb punishment and still fly, a con-

fidence builder for its hard-pressed pilots. The Wildcat was also a tough little fighter ("built like Grumman iron" was a popular catch-phrase of the period), and had a devastating battery of four (for the F4F-3) or six .50-caliber machine guns (for the F4F-4) and a fair degree of maneuverability.

Both the Imperial Japanese Army and Navy also had outstanding aircraft. The Army's primary fighter of the early war was the Nakajima K.43 Hayabusa (Peregrine Falcon), a light, little aircraft, with a slim, tapered fuselage and a bubble canopy.

The Navy's fighter came to symbolize the Japanese air effort, even for the Japanese, themselves. The Mitsubishi Type "O" Carrier Fighter (its official designation) was as much a trend-setting design as was Britain's Spitfire or the American Corsair.

However, as author Norman Franks wrote, the Allied crews found that "the Japanese airmen were...far superior to the crude stereotypes so disparaged by the popular press and cartoonists. And in a Zero they were highly dangerous."

The hallmark of Japanese fighters had always been superb maneuverability. Early biplanes—which had been developed from British and French designs—set the pace. By the mid-1930s, the Army and Navy had two world-class fighters, the Nakajima Ki.27 and the Mitsubishi A5M series, respectively, both low-wing, fixed-gear aircraft. The Ki.27 did have a modern enclosed cockpit, while the A5M's cockpit was open (except for one variant that experimented with a canopy

The first production model of Grumman's stubby, little Wildcat was the F4F-3, which carried four .50-caliber machine guns in the wings. Its wings did not fold, unlike the -4 which added two more machine guns and folding wings. These F4F-3s of VMF-121 carry prewar exercise markings.

Author's Collection

The Wildcat was a relatively small aircraft, as were most of the prewar fighters throughout the world. The aircraft's narrow gear track is shown to advantage in this ground view of a VMF-121 F4F-3.

This A6M3 is taking off from Rabaul in 1943.

Brewster's fat little F2A Buffalo is credited with a dismal performance in American and British service, although the Finns racked up a fine score against the Russians. This view of a Marine Brewster shows the aptness of its popular name, which actually came from the British. Its characteristic greenhouse canopy and main wheels tucked snugly into its belly are also well shown.

which was soon discarded in service.) A major and fatal disadvantage of most Japanese fighters was their light armament—usually a pair of .30-caliber machine guns—and lack of armor, as well as their great flammability.

When the Type "0" first flew in 1939, most Japanese pilots were enthusiastic about the new fighter. It was fast, had retractable landing gear and an enclosed cockpit, and carried two 20mm cannon besides the two machine guns. Initial operational evaluation in China in 1940 confirmed the aircraft's potential.

By the time of the Japanese attack on Pearl Harbor, the A6M2 was the Imperial Navy's standard carrier fighter, and rapidly replaced the older A5Ms still in service. As the A6M2 proved successful in combat, it acquired its wartime nickname, "Zero," although the Japanese rarely referred to it as such. The evocative name came from the custom of designating aircraft in

The Zero's incredible maneuverability came at some expense from its top speed. In an effort to increase the speed, the designers clipped the folding wingtips from the carrier-based A6M2 and evolved the land-based A6M3, Model 32. The pilots were not impressed with the speed increase and the production run was short, the A6M3 reverting back to its span as the Model 22. The type was originally called "Hap," after Gen Henry "Hap" Arnold, Chief of the Army Air Force. Arnold was so angry at the dubious honor that the name was quickly changed to Hamp. This Hamp is shown in the Solomons during the Guadalcanal campaign.

reference to the Japanese calendar. Thus, since 1940 corresponded to the year 2600 in Japan, the fighter was the Type "00" fighter, which was shortened to "0." The western press picked up the designation and the name "Zero" was born.

The fighter received another name in 1943 which was almost as popular, especially among the American flight crews. A system of first names referred to various enemy aircraft, in much the same way that the postwar NATO system referred to Soviet and Chinese aircraft. The Zero was tagged "Zeke," and the names were used interchangeably by everyone, from flight crews to intelligence officers. (Other examples of the system included "Claude" [A5M], "Betty" [Mitsubishi G4M bomber], and "Oscar" [Ki.43].)

As discussed in the main text, the Navy and Marine Corps Wildcats were sometimes initially hard-pressed to defend their ships and fields against the large forces of Betty bombers and their Zero escorts, which had ranges of 800 miles or more through the use of drop tanks.

The Brewster Buffalo had little to show for its few encounters with the Japanese, which is difficult to understand given the type's early success during the Russo-Finnish War. The F2A-1, a lighter, earlier model of the -3 which served with the Marines, was the standard Finnish fighter plane. In its short combat career in American service, the Brewster failed miserably.

Thus, the only fighter capable of meeting the Japanese on anything approaching equal terms was the F4F, which was fortunate because the Wildcat was really all that was available in those dark days following Pearl Harbor. Retired Brigadier General Robert E. Galer described the Wildcat as "very rugged and very mistreated (at Guadalcanal)." He added:

The A6M2-N floatplane version of the Zero did fairly well, suffering only a small loss in its legendary maneuverability. Top speed was somewhat affected, however, and the aircraft's relatively light armament was a detriment.

Full throttle, very few replacement parts, muddy landing strips, battle damage, roughly repaired. We loved them. We did not worry about flight characteristics except when senior officers wanted to make them bombers as well as fighters.

The Japanese also operated a unique form of fighter. Other combatants had tried to make seaplanes of existing designs. The U.S. Navy had even hung floats on the Wildcat, which quickly became the "Wildcatfish." The British had done it with the Spitfire. But the resulting combination left much to be desired and sapped the original design of much of its speed and maneuverability.

The Japanese, however, seeing the need for a water-based fighter in the expanses of the Pacific, modified the A6M2 Zero, and came up with what was arguably the most successful water-based fighter

of the war, the A6M2-N, which was allocated the Allied codename "Rufe."

Manufactured by Mitsubishi's competitor, Nakajima, float-Zeros served in such disparate climates as the Aleutians and the Solomons. Although the floats bled off at least 40 mph from the land-based version's top speed, they seemed to have had only a minor effect on its original maneuverability; the Rufe aquired the same respect as its sire.

While the F4F and P-40 (along with the luckless P-39) held the line in the Pacific, other, newer designs were leaving production lines, and none too soon. The two best newcomers were the Army's Lockheed P-38 Lightning and the Navy's Vought F4U Corsair. The P-38 quickly captured the headlines and public interest with its unique twin-boomed, twin-engine layout. It soon developed into a long-range escort, and served in the Pacific as well as Europe.

The Corsair was originally intended to fly from aircraft carriers, but its high landing speed, long nose that obliterated the pilot's view forward during the landing approach, and its tendency to bounce, banished the big fighter from American flight decks for a while. The British, however, modified the aircraft, mainly by clipping its wings, and flew it from their small decks.

Deprived of its new carrier fighter—having settled on the new Grumman F6F Hellcat as its main carrier fighter—the Navy offered the F4U to the Marines. They took the first squadrons to the Solomons, and after a few disappointing first missions, they made the gull-winged fighter their own, eventually even flying it from the small decks of Navy escort carriers in the later stages of the war.

A good view of an early F4U-1 under construction in 1942. The massive amount of wiring and piping for the aircraft's huge Pratt & Whitney engine shows up here, as do the Corsair's gull wings.

The Marine pilot of this F4U-1, Lt Donald Balch, contemplates his good fortune by the damaged tail of his fighter. The Corsair was a relatively tough aircraft, but like any plane, damage to vital portions of its controls or powerplant could prove fatal.

National Archives 80G-54284

This "bird-cage" Corsair is landing at Espiritu Santo in September 1943. The aircraft's paint is well-weathered and its main gear tires are "dusty" from the coral runways of the area.

National Archives 80G-54279

Besides the two main fighters, the Army's Oscar and the Navy's Zeke and its floatplane derivative, the Rufe, the Japanese flew a wide assortment of aircraft, including land-based bombers, such as the Mitsubishi G4M (codenamed Betty) and Ki.21 (Sally). Carrier-based bombers included the Aichi D3A divebomber (the Val) which saw considerable service during the first three years of the war, and its stablemate, the torpedo bomber from Nakajima, the B5N (Kate), one of the most capable torpedo-carriers of the first half of the war. The Marine Corps squadrons in the Solomons regularly encountered these aircraft. First Lieutenant James Swett's two engagements on 7 April 1943 netted the young Wildcat pilot seven Vals, and the Medal of Honor.

Although early wartime propaganda ridiculed Japanese aircraft and their pilots, returning Allied aviators told different stories, although the details of their experiences were kept classified. Each side's culture provided the basis for their aircraft design

Mitsubishi G4M Betty bombers, perhaps during the Solomons campaign. Probably the best Japanese land-based bomber in the war's first two years, the G4M series enjoyed a long range,

1stLt Rolland N. Rinabarger of VMF-214 in his early F4U-1 Corsair at Espiritu Santo in September 1943. Badly shot up by Zeros during an early mission to Kahili only two weeks after this photo was taken. Lt Rinabarger returned to the States for lengthy treatment. He was still in California when the war ended. The national insignia on his Corsair is outlined in red, a short-lived attempt to regain that color from the prewar marking after the red circle was deleted following Pearl Harbor to avoid confusion with the Japanese "meatball." Even this small amount of red was deceptive, however, and by mid-1944, it was gone from the insignia again. Note the large mud spray on the aft under fuselage.

philosophies. Eventually, the Japanese were overwhelmed by American technology and numerical superiority. However, for the important first 18 months of the Pacific war, they had the best. But, as was also the case in the European theaters, a series of misfortunes, coincidences, a lack of understanding by leaders, as well as the drain of prolonged combat, finally allowed the Americans and their Allies to overcome the enemy's initial edge.

but could burst into flames under attack, much to the chagrin of its crews. The type flew as a suicide aircraft, and finally, painted white with green crosses, carried surrender teams to various sites.

Photo courtesy Robert Mikesh

Galer would also be shot down three more times during his flying career—twice more during World War II and once during a tour in Korea.

The last half of September 1942 was a time of extreme trial for the Cactus Air Force (Cactus was the codename for Guadalcanal). Some relief for the Marine squadrons came in the form of bad weather and the arrival of disjointed contingents of Navy aircraft and crews who were displaced from carriers which were either sunk, or damaged. *Saratoga* (CV3) and *Enterprise* (CV6) had been torpedoed or bombed and sent back to rear area repair stations. The remaining carriers, *Hornet* (CV8) and *Wasp* (CV7), patrolled off Guadalcanal, their captains and admirals decidedly uneasy about exposing the last American flattops in the Pacific as meaty targets to the numerically superior Japanese ships and aircraft.

Wasp took a lurking Japanese submarine's torpedoes on 15 September while covering a convoy. Now only *Hornet* remained. Navy planes and crews from *Enterprise*, *Saratoga*, and now *Wasp* flew into Henderson Field to supplement the hard-pressed Marine fighter and bomber squadrons there. It was still a meager force of 63 barely operational aircraft, a collection of Navy and Marine F4Fs and SBDs, Navy Grumman TBF Avenger torpedo bombers, and a few forlorn Army P-400s. A few new Marine pilots from VMF-121 filtered in on 25 September. However, two days later, the crews from *Enterprise's* contingent took their planes out to meet their carrier steaming in to arrive on station off Guadalcanal. As the weather broke on the 27th, the *Enterprise* crews took their leave of Guadalcanal.

The next day, the Japanese mounted their first raid in nearly two weeks. Warned by the coast-watchers, Navy and Marine fighters rose to intercept the 70-plane force. Now a lieutenant colonel, Harold "Indian Joe" Bauer was making one of his periodic visits from Efate, and scored a kill, a Zero, before landing.

A native of North Platte, Nebraska, Bauer was part-Indian (as was Major Gregory "Pappy" Boyington). A veteran of 10 years as a Marine aviator, he watched the progress of the campaign at Guadalcanal from his rear-area base on Efate. He would come north, using as an excuse the need to check on those members of his squadron who had been sent to Henderson and would occasionally fly with the Cactus fighters.

His victory on the 28th was his first, and soon, Bauer was a familiar face to the Henderson crews. Bauer was visiting VMF-224 on 3 October when a coastwatcher reported a large group of Japanese bombers inbound for Henderson. VMF-223 and -224 took off to intercept the raiders. The Marine Wildcats accounted for 11 enemy aircraft; Lieutenant Colonel Bauer claimed four, making him an ace.

On 30 September, Admiral Chester Nimitz, Commander-in-Chief, Pacific, braved a heavy rainstorm to fly in to Henderson for an awards ceremony. John Smith, Marion Carl, and Bob Galer, as well as some 1st Marine Division personnel, received the Navy Cross. Other members of the Cactus Air Force, Navy and Marine, were decorated with Distinguished Flying Crosses. Nimitz departed in a blinding rain after presenting a total of 27 medals to the men of the Cactus Air Force.

Combat in October

October was a pivotal month for the air campaign on Guadalcanal. It was a time when the men who had arrived in August were clearly at the end of their endurance, for sick-ness and fatigue hit them after they had survived Japanese bullets. However, new squadrons and crews were arriving, among them VMF-121, led by Major Leonard K. "Duke" Davis. His executive officer, Captain Joseph J. Foss, would soon make a name for himself.

Foss came from Sioux Falls, South Dakota, and as a boy had developed a shooting eye which would stand him in good stead over Guadalcanal. He enlisted in the Marine Corps in February 1940 and received his wings of gold 13 months later. Originally considered too old to fly fighters (he was 27), he was ordered to a photo reconnaissance squadron in San Diego. However, he kept submitting requests for transfer to fighters and was finally sent to VMF-121.

A few days after arriving at Henderson, Foss scored his first victory on 13 October. As an attacking Zero fired and missed, Foss fired his guns sending the enemy fighter down. Three more Zeros then attacked Foss, putting holes in his Wildcat's oil system. The newly blooded pilot had to make a dead-stick landing back at Cactus Base.

Other veterans of the campaign had not stayed idle. Major Smith of VMF-223 had taken his squadron up on 2 October against a raid by Japanese bombers and fighters. The Zero escorts dove on the climbing Navy and Marine Wildcats, quickly shooting down two fighters from VMF-223. Smith exited a cloud to confront three Zeros. He blasted a fighter into a ball of flame. However, the two remaining Zeros got on his tail and peppered the struggling little blue-gray F4F with cannon and machine gun fire. Listening to a repaired radio from a damaged SBD back at Guadalcanal, the crews of Dennis Byrd's VMSB-232 heard Captain Carl call to his skipper. "John, you've got a Zero on your tail!" "I know, I know," Smith replied, "shoot the SOB if you can!" Then all was silence.

Smith's aircraft was mortally wounded, and he tried to regain the field. He finally had to make a dead-stick landing six miles from the strip and walk back, watching all the time for roving Japanese patrols.

Second Lieutenant Charles H. Kendrick was not as fortunate as his skipper. The Zeros had gotten him on their first pass, and he tried to guide his stricken fighter to a crash landing. He apparently landed close to Henderson, but his fighter flipped over on its back, killing the young pilot.

Major Smith led a party to the crash site. They found Kendrick still in his cockpit. They released and buried him beside his plane. Stan Nicolay recalled, "I don't know how many we lost that day. We really took a beating." Actually, six Wildcats had been shot down or returned with strike damage. Several others required major repair.

VMF-224's skipper was also shot down. Bob Galer bailed out over the water—his third shootdown in less than three weeks—and was rescued. He had accounted for two Zeros, however. He recalled:

I was up with six fighters, cruising about at 20,000 or 25,000 feet. Suddenly, 18 Zeros came at us out of the sun, and we took 'em on. The day was cloudy and after a few minutes, the only other Marine I could find was Second Lieutenant Dean Hartley. In the melee of first contact, I heard several Jap bullets splatter against—and through—my ship, but none stopped me. At about the same moment, Hartley and I started to climb into a group of seven Zeros hovering above us. In about four minutes, I shot down two Zeros and Hartley got a possible. The other four were just too many and we were both shot down. Hartley got to a field, but I couldn't make it. The Jap that got me really had me boresighted. He raked my ship from wingtip to wingtip. He blasted the rudder bar right from under my foot. My cockpit was so perforated it's a miracle that I escaped. The blast drove the rivets from the pedal into my leg. I pancaked into the water near Florida Island. It took me an hour-and-a-half to swim ashore….I worried not only about the Japs but about the tide turning against me, and sharks.

Major Galer struggled ashore where he encountered four men armed with machetes and spears. Fortunately, the natives were friendly and took the bedraggled pilot to their village. After enjoying what hospitality his hosts could offer, Major Galer rode in a native canoe to a Marine camp on a beach five miles away. He made his way back to Henderson from there.

Marine Aircraft Group 23 and the rest of its squadrons also left the following day, having earned a rest from the intense combat of the last two-and-a-half months. Between 20 August and 16 October, the squadrons of MAG-23 and attached Army and Navy squadrons had shot down 244 Japanese aircraft, including 111.5 by VMF-223 and 60.5 by VMF-224. The score had not come free, though. Twenty-two pilots of the group, as well as 33 aviators from other Navy, Marine, and Army squadrons assigned to the Cactus Air Force, had been lost.

John Smith had seen his last engagement. He received the Medal of Honor for his leadership during the Guadalcanal campaign and finished the war as the sixth highest on the

Maj John L. Smith, LtCol Richard C. Mangrum, and Capt Marion E. Carl pose for photos after returning to the States. LtCol Mangrum commanded an SBD squadron at the height of the Cactus campaign and was universally admired. He eventually attained the rank of lieutenant general, while Marion Carl retired as a major general after fighting in three wars—World War II, the Korean War, and the Vietnam War.

Department of Defense photo (USMC) A707812

Painting by William S. Phillips, courtesy of The Greenwich Workshop

Marion Carl, now a major and commanding his old squadron, VMF-223, made his 17th kill in December 1943, when he shot down a Japanese Tony over Rabaul. Carl was escorting Marine PBJ (B-25) bombers in his F4U-1 Corsair when the enemy fighter jumped the raiders. The victory was Carl's next-to-last score.

list of Marine Corps aces, closely followed by his friend and rival, Marion Carl. Much to his initial chagrin, Smith found himself on the War Bond circuit, and then training new pilots. It was not until two years later, in 1944, that Lieutenant Colonel Smith got a combat assignment again. As commanding officer of MAG-32 in Hawaii, he took the group to Bougainville and the Philippines.

Marion Carl assumed command of his old squadron, VMF-223, in the United States in January 1943 and took the newly renamed Bulldogs to the South Pacific late in the fall. He gained two more kills—a Ki.61 Tony (a Japanese Army fighter) and a Zero, on 23 December and 27 December 1943, respectively—this time in a Vought F4U Corsair. His final score at the end of the war was 18.5 Japanese aircraft destroyed.

The night of 13-14 October saw the Japanese pound beleaguered Henderson Field with every gun they could fire from their assembled flotilla offshore, as well as the entrenched artillery positions hidden in the dense jungle surrounding the field. The night-long barrage might very well have been the end for the Cactus Marines.

The new day revealed that of 39 Dauntlesses, only seven could be considered operational, only a few Army fighters could stagger into the air, and all the TBF Avenger torpedo bombers were destroyed or down. The only saving factor was that the fighter strip was relatively untouched. By the afternoon, a few Wildcats were sent up to mount a patrol over Henderson while it pulled itself together. For the next few days, the Cactus Air Force—Marine, Navy, and Army—flew as though its collective life was on the line, which it was.

Although VMF-223 had left, Guadalcanal still had several top scoring aces left, among them Captain Joe Foss of VMF-121 and Lieutenant Colonel Harold Bauer of VMF-212. Throughout October 1942, Foss and Bauer were kept busy by constant Japanese raids, desperately trying to dislodge the determined Marines from the island.

Lieutenant Colonel Bauer had led his VMF-212 up from Espiritu Santo on the afternoon of 16 October, when he finally had his own squadron at Henderson. With empty gas tanks, the 18 Wildcats were running on fumes as they entered the landing pattern in time to see a U.S. transport under attack from Japanese dive-bombers. Without hesitating, Bauer broke from the pattern and charged into the Vals, shooting down four of them. It was an incredible way to advertise the arrival of his squadron.

Joe Foss took off on the afternoon of 23 October to intercept an incoming force of Betty bombers, escorted by Zeros. Five of the escorting fighters dove toward Foss and his flight, followed by 20 more Zeros. Diving to gain speed, the VMF-121 executive officer saw a Wildcat pursued by a Zero. He fired at the Japanese fighter, shredding it with his six .50-caliber machine guns.

Without losing speed, Foss racked his aircraft into a loop behind another Zero. He destroyed this second Mitsubishi while both fighters hung inverted over Guadalcanal. As he came out of the loop, Foss hit a third Zero. A fourth kill finished off a highly productive mission.

On 25 October, Foss took off again against a Japanese raid, and this time, he shot down two enemy aircraft. Later the same day, Foss gunned down three more Zeros for a total of five in one day, and an overall score of 16 kills.

Marine Corps Aviators Who Received the Medal of Honor in World War II

Of the 81 Medals of Honor awarded to Marines for service during World War II, 11 Marine Corps aviators received America's highest military award. Except for two posthumous awards, the medals all went to aces who served in the Solomons and Bougainville campaigns. The Medal of Honor was awarded to Captain Henry T. Elrod of VMF-211 and Captain Richard E. Fleming of VMSB-241. Captain Elrod was killed on Wake in December 1941. Although his award is chronologically the first Medal of Honor to be awarded to a Marine during the war, his performance did not become known until survivors of Wake had been repatriated after the war.

Captain Fleming was a dive-bomber pilot at Midway in 1942. VMSB-241 flew both the obsolete Vought SB2U Vindicator and the SBD Dauntless during this pivotal battle. On 5 June 1942, Captain Fleming was last seen diving on a Japanese ship amidst a wall of flak. His Vindicator struck the cruiser's aft turret.

Two of the remaining nine awards were for specific actions; the other seven were for periods of continued service or more than one mission. Seven of these awards were for service in the Solomons-Guadalcanal Campaign. The awards for specific actions went to First Lieutenant Jefferson DeBlanc (31 January 1943) and First Lieutenant James E. Swett (7 April 1943).

Five of these awards were originally posthumous. However, Major Gregory Boyington made a surprise return from captivity as a prisoner of war to receive his award in person from President Harry S. Truman.

The Pilots and Their Aircraft

*Lieutenant Colonel Harold W. Bauer, VMF-212. For service from May to November 1942. Grumman F4F-4 Wildcat.

Major Gregory Boyington, VMF-214. For service from September 1943 to January 1944 in the Central Solomons. Vought F4U-1/F4U-1A Corsair.

First Lieutenant Jefferson J. DeBlanc, VMF-112. For action on 31 January 1943. Grumman F4F-4 Wildcat.

*Captain Henry T. Elrod, VMF-211. For action on Wake Island 8-23 December 1941. Grumman F4F-3 Wildcat.

*Captain Richard E. Fleming, VMSB-241. For action at the Battle of Midway, 4-5 June 1942. Vought SB2U-3 Vindicator.

Captain Joseph J. Foss, VMF-121. For service in the Guadalcanal Campaign, October 1942-January 1943. Grumman F4F-4 Wildcat.

Major Robert E. Galer, VMF-224. For service in the Guadalcanal Campaign, August-September 1942. Grumman F4F-4 Wildcat.

*First Lieutenant Robert M. Hanson, VMF-215. For action in the Central Solomons, November 1943 and January 1944. Vought F4U-1 Corsair.

Major Robert L. Smith, VMF-223. For service in the Guadalcanal Campaign, August-September 1942. Grumman F4F-4 Wildcat.

First Lieutenant James E. Swett, VMF-221. For action on 7 April 1943 over Guadalcanal. Grumman F4F-4 Wildcat.

First Lieutenant Kenneth A. Walsh, VMF-124. For action on 15 and 30 August 1943. Vought F4U-1 Corsair.

*indicates a posthumous award

Lieutenant Colonel Bauer was adding to his score, too. A veteran aviator, Colonel Bauer was a respected flight leader. He frequently gave pep talks to his younger pilots, earning the affectionate nickname of "Coach." Bauer had taken over as commander of fighters on Guadalcanal on 23 October.

Before the big mission on 23 October, the Coach had told his pilots, "When you see Zeros, dogfight 'em!" His instructions went against the warnings that most of American fighter pilots had been given about the lithe little Japanese fighter. Joe Foss' success on this day seemed to vindicate Bauer, however. Twenty Zeros and two Bettys, including the four Zeros claimed by Foss, went down in front of Marine Wildcats.

Up to this time the Zero was considered the best fighter in the Pacific. This belief stemmed from the fact that the Zero had spectacular characteristics of performance in both maneuverability, rate of climb, and radius of action, all first noted at the Battles of the Coral Sea and Midway. And it was because of its performances in these actions that it achieved the seeming invincibility that it did. At the same time, the Zero was highly flammable because it lacked armor plate in any form in its design and also because it had no self-sealing fuel tanks, such as existed in U.S. aircraft. Initially in the war, in the hands of a good pilot, the Zero could usually take care of itself against its heavier and tougher American opponents, but early in the air battles over Guadalcanal, its days of supremacy became numbered. By the end of the war in the Pacific, the kill ratio of U.S. planes over Japanese aircraft went from approximately 2.5:1 to better than 10:1.

What made the difference as far as Lieutenant Colonel Bauer was concerned was his feeling that, in the 10 months of intense combat

after Pearl Harbor, including their disastrous and failed adventure at Midway, the Japanese had lost many of their most experienced pilots, and their replacements were neither so good nor experienced. Many of the major aces of the Zero squadrons—the ones who had accumulated many combat hours over China—had, indeed, been lost or been rotated out of the combat zone. Whatever the situation, most of the Marine pilots in this early part of the war in the South Pacific would still admit that the Japanese remained a force to be reckoned with.

The Japanese endeavored to reassert their dominance on 25 October. In a last-ditch effort to remove American carriers from the South Pacific, a fleet including three aircraft carriers sortied to find the U.S. carriers *Enterprise* and *Hornet*, all that remained at the moment of the meager U.S. carrier strength in the Pacific.

The Japanese fleet was discovered during an intensive search by PBY flying boats, and the battle was joined early in the morning of 26

October. What became known as the Battle of Santa Cruz occurred some 300 miles southeast of Guadalcanal. Indeed, most of the Marine and Navy flight crews attempting to blunt remaining enemy air raids still plaguing the positions of the embattled ground forces on Guadalcanal had no idea that another desperate fight was being waged that would have a distinct impact on their situation back at Henderson.

Many American Navy flight crews received their baptism of fire during Santa Cruz. *Hornet* was hit by Japanese dive-bombers and eventually abandoned—one of the few times that a still-floating American ship had been left to the enemy, even though she was burning from stem to stern. (The carrier was only a year old.) *Enterprise* was hit by Val dive-bombers, and the aircraft of her Air Group 10 were ultimately forced to land on Guadalcanal. The displaced Navy crews remained at Henderson until 10 November, while their ship underwent repairs at Noumea, New Caledonia.

While the Marines on Guadalcanal fought for their lives, their Navy compatriots far offshore also challenged the Japanese. At the Battle of Santa Cruz, October 1942, Japanese bombers hit the American ships, damaging the vital carrier Enterprise *as well as attacking squadrons of inexperienced Navy aircrews. This A6M2 Model 21 Zero launches from the carrier* Sholalu *during Santa Cruz while deck crewmen cheer on the pilot, Lt Hideki Shingo.*
Author's Collection

While blame and recriminations went the rounds of the Navy's Pacific commands—for it seemed that Santa Cruz was a debacle, a strategic and tactical defeat for the hard-pressed carrier force—the effects of the battle would become clear soon.

Sixty-nine Japanese aircraft had been shot down by Navy F4Fs and antiaircraft fire. An additional 23 were forced to ditch because of crippling battle damage.

Like Midway, Santa Cruz deprived the Japanese of many of their vital aircraft *and* their experienced flight crews and flight commanders. Thus, as the frantic month of October gave way to November, and although they did not know it at the time, the Cactus Air Force crews had been given a respite, and

Brigadier General Roy S. Geiger, USMC

General Geiger, commander of the 1st Marine Aircraft Wing, arrived on Guadalcanal on 3 September 1942 to assume command of air operations emanating from Henderson Field. He was 57 years old, and he had been a Marine for 35 of those years, commanded a squadron in France in World War I, served a number of tours fighting the bandits in Central America, and had served in the Philippines and China. He was designated a naval aviator in June 1917, thus becoming the fifth flyer in the Marine Corps and the 49th in the naval service. In the course of his career, he had a number of assignments to staff and command billets as well as tours at senior military courses such as the ones at the Army Command and Staff School at Fort Leavenworth, the Army War College at Carlisle, and the Navy War College at Newport. He also was both a student and instructor at various times at the Marine Corps Schools, Quantico, Virginia. Among other reasons, it was because of his sound training in strategy and tactics at these schools and his long experience as a Marine that he was so well equipped to assume command of I Marine Amphibious Corps (later III Amphibious

Corps) for the Bougainville, Guam, Peleliu, and Okinawa operations.

When Lieutenant General Simon Bolivar Buckner, Jr., USA, commander of the Tenth Army on Okinawa was killed, and based on General Buckner's stated decision before the operation, General Geiger took over command and became the first Marine ever to accede to command of as large a unit as an army. He was then 60, an age when many men in civilian life looked forward to retirement.

But it was at Guadalcanal, where his knowledge of Marine planes and pilots was so important in defeating the myth of Japanese invincibility in the air, that he first made his mark in the Pacific War. A short, husky, tanned, and white-haired Marine, whose deep blue eyes were piercing and whose reputation had preceded him, compelled instant attention, recognition, and dedication on the part of his junior pilots, many of whom had but a few hours of experience in the planes they were flying. As told in this pamphlet, out of meager beginnings grew the reputation and success in combat of the aces in the Solomons.

—Benis M. Frank

ultimately, the key to victory over the island.

Meanwhile, under the command of Admiral Isoroku Yamamoto, the Japanese decided to make one more try to land troops and material on Guadalcanal and to regain the island and its airstrips. The Americans were also bringing new squadrons and men in to fortify Cactus Base and Henderson Field. MAG-11 arrived on 1 November, bringing the SBDs of VMSB-132 and the F4Fs of VMF-112. Newly promoted Brigadier General Louis Woods arrived on 7 November to relieve Brigadier General Roy S. Geiger as commander of the Cactus Air Force. Both men were pioneer Marine aviators, and Geiger had led his squadrons through some of the most intense combat to be seen during the war. But, almost inevitably, the strain was beginning to show on the tough, 57-year-old Geiger. He had once taken off in an SBD in full view of his troops and dropped a 1,000-pound bomb on a Japanese position, showing his troops that a former squadron commander in France in World War I could still do it.

As new planes and crews arrived at Henderson and the frustrated Japanese planned their final attacks, the Cactus Marines fought on. On 7 November, a sighting of a force of Japanese ships near Florida Island scrambled a strike group of SBDs and their F4F escorts. Captain Joe Foss led eight VMF-121 Wildcats, each with 250-pound bombs beneath its wings. The VMSB-132 Dauntlesses carried 500-pounders in their centerline-mounted bomb racks.

The heavily laden aircraft took some 30 minutes to climb to 12,000 feet as their crews searched for the enemy flotilla. As he looked ahead and below, Foss spotted six Japanese floatplane Zeros—a modification of the A6M2 model of the land-

Painting by Ted Wilbur, courtesy of the artist

Using hit-and-run tactics, Capt Joe Foss flames a Japanese Zero over Henderson Field in October 1942.

and carrier-based Zero—crossing from right to left, descending. Alerting his squadron mates, he dropped his light bombs and headed toward the unsuspecting enemy fighters.

In one slashing pass, Foss' Wildcats shot down five of the six Zeros, Foss' target literally disintegrating under the weight of his heavy machine gun fire. One of the other Wildcats shot down the surviving Zero. All six enemy pilots bailed out of their fighters and seemed to be out of danger as they floated toward the water. As the incredulous Marine pilots watched, however, the six Japanese aviators unlatched their parachute harnesses and fell to their deaths.

Foss called for his fighters to regroup in preparation for a strafing run on the enemy warships below. He spotted a slow float biplane—probably a Mitsubishi type used for reconnaissance—and lined up for what he thought would be an easy kill. However, the two-seater was surprisingly maneuverable, and its pilot chopped the throttle, letting his rear gunner get a good shot at the surprised American fighter.

The gunner's aim was good and Foss' Wildcat suffered heavy damage before he finally dispatched the audacious little floatplane. Soon, the VMF-121 executive officer found a third victim, another floatplane, and shot it down. Regrouping with a portion of his group, he flew back to Henderson Field with another badly damaged Wildcat. However, the two cripples were spotted en route by enemy fighters. The two American fighters tried to get to the protection of clouds. Foss succeeded, but his wingman was apparently shot down by the enemy flight.

Foss was not out of danger, however, as his engine finally quit, forcing him to glide toward the sea, 3,500 feet below. He dropped through heavy rain, trying to gauge the best way to put his aircraft down in the water. He spotted a small village on the coast of a nearby island and wondered if the natives would turn him over to the Japanese.

He hit the water with enough force to slam his canopy shut, momentarily trapping him in the cockpit as the Wildcat began to sink. In a few seconds which seemed like an

Two aces walk with another famous aviator. Charles Lindbergh, right, visited the Pacific combat areas several times to help Army, Navy, and Marine Corps squadrons get the most from the respective mounts. Here, the pioneer transatlantic flier visits with now-Maj Joe Foss, left, and now-Maj Marion Carl, center, in May 1944.

eternity, he struggled to free himself from his seat and the straps of his parachute, and force the canopy open again. His aircraft was well below the surface and only after an adrenalin-charged push, was he able to ram the canopy back and shoot from his plane. He remembered to inflate his Mae West life preserver, which helped him get to the surface where he lay gasping for air.

After floating for a long time as darkness fell, Foss was finally rescued by natives and a missionary priest from the village he had seen as he dropped toward the water. The rescue came none too soon as sharks, which frequented the waters near the island, had begun to appear around the Marine pilot.

A PBY flew up from Henderson the next day to collect him and he was back in action the day after he returned. On 12 November, he scored three kills, making him the top American ace of the war, and the first to reach 20 kills.

The Battle for Guadalcanal

On the night of 12-13 November, American and Japanese naval forces fought a classic naval battle which has been called the First Battle of Guadalcanal. It was a tactical defeat for the Americans who lost two rear admirals killed in action on the bridges of their respective flagships.

The next day, 14 November, the Second Battle of Guadalcanal pitted aircraft from the carrier *Enterprise* and Henderson Field against a large enemy force trying to run the Slot, the body of water running down the Solomons chain between Guadalcanal and New Georgia. By midnight, another naval engagement was underway. This battle turned out differently for the Japanese, who lost several ships, including 10 transports carrying more than 4,000 troops and their equipment.

The Navy and Marines from *Enterprise* and Henderson hammered the enemy ships, while the Americans on the island, in turn, were harassed day and night by well-entrenched enemy artillery positions still on Guadalcanal and the huge guns of the Japanese battleships and cruisers offshore.

During these furious engagements, Lieutenant Colonel Bauer had dutifully stayed on the ground, organizing Cactus air strikes and ordering other people into the air. Finally, on the afternoon of 14 November, Colonel Bauer scheduled himself to lead seven F4Fs from VMF-121 as escorts for a strike by SBDs and TBFs against the Japanese transport ships.

Together with Captain Foss and Second Lieutenant Thomas W. "Coot" Furlow, Bauer strafed one of the transports before turning back for Henderson. Two Zeros sneaked up on the Marine fighters, but Bauer turned to meet the

threat, shooting down one of the Japanese attackers. The second Zero dragged Foss and Furlow over a Japanese destroyer which did its best to take out the Wildcats. By the time they had shaken the Zero and returned to the point where they last saw the Coach, they found a large oil slick with Colonel Bauer in the middle, wearing his yellow Mae West, waving furiously at his squadron mates.

Foss quickly flew back to Henderson and jumped into a Grumman Duck, a large amphibian used as a hack transport and rescue vehicle. Precious time was lost as the Duck had to hold for a squadron of Army B-26 bombers landing after a flight from New Caledonia; they were nearly out of gas. Finally, Foss and the Duck's pilot, Lieutenant Joseph N. Renner, roared off in the last light of the day. By the time they arrived over Bauer's last position, it was dark and the Coach was nowhere to be seen.

The next morning a desperate search found nothing of Lieutenant Colonel Bauer. He was never found and was presumed to have drowned or have been attacked by the sharks which were a constant threat to all aviators forced to parachute into the waters around Guadalcanal during the campaign.

Bauer's official score of 11 Japanese aircraft destroyed (revised lists credit him with 10) did not begin to tell the impact the loss the tough veteran had on the young Marine and Navy crews at Henderson. He was decorated with a Medal of Honor posthumously for his flight on 16 October, when he shot down four Japanese Val dive-bombers, but the high award could also be considered as having been given in recognition of his leadership of his own squadron, VMF-212, and later, as the commander of the fighters of the Cactus Air Force.

Painting by William S. Phillips, courtesy of The Greenwich Workshop

Capt Foss saves a fellow pilot by shooting down an attacking Zero during an engagement on 23 October 1942.

The loss of the Coach was a hard blow. Another loss, albeit temporary, was that of Joe Foss who became severely ill with malaria. (Many of the Cactus Air Force aviators, like the ground troops, battled one tropical malady or another during their combat tours.) Foss flew out to New Caledonia on 19 November with a temperature of 104 degrees. He spent the next month on sick leave, also losing 37 pounds. While in Australia, he met some of the Australian pilots who had flown against Nazi pilots in the Desert War in North Africa. In one of his conversations with them, he told the Aussies, "We have a saying up at Guadalcanal, if you're alone and you meet a Zero, run like hell because you're outnumbered." In

the coming months, they would find out he knew was he was talking about.

Foss returned to Guadalcanal on 31 December 1942, and remained on combat status until 17 February 1943, when he was ordered back to the U.S. By this time, besides enduring several return bouts with malaria, he had shot down another six Japanese aircraft for a final total of 26 aircraft and no balloons, thus becoming the first American pilot to equal the score of Captain Edward Rickenbacker, the top U.S. ace in World War I. In that war, tethered balloons shot down counted as aircraft splashed. Of the 26 planes Rickenbacker was given credit for, four were balloons.

Joe Foss was one of the Cactus

Marines who was awarded the Medal of Honor for his cumulative work during their intense campaign. Summoned to the White House on 18 May 1943, he was decorated by President Franklin D. Roosevelt. After his action-packed tour at Guadalcanal, Captain Foss went on the requisite War Bond tour. Promoted to major, he took command of a new fighter squadron, VMF-115, equipped with F4U-1 Corsairs.

Originally nicknamed "Joe's Jokers," in deference to their famous skipper, VMF-115 flew a short combat tour from Bougainville during May when there was little or no enemy air activity from and above Rabaul. Major Foss did not add to his score.

Cactus Victory

By Christmas 1942, the Japanese position was clearly untenable. Their troops who remained on Guadalcanal were sick and short of food, medicine, and ammunition. There was still plenty of action on the ground and in the air, but not like the intense engagements of the previous fall. On 31 January 1943, First Lieutenant Jefferson J. DeBlanc of VMF-112 led six Wildcats as escorts for a strike by Dauntlesses and Avengers. He encountered a strong force of Zeros near Kolombangara Island and took his fighters down to meet the threat before the Japanese could reach the Marine bombers.

In a wild melee, DeBlanc, who already had three Zeros to his credit, shot down three more before hearing a call for help from the bombers now under attack by floatplane Zeros. DeBlanc and his flight climbed back to the formation and dispersed the float Zeros.

Soon after the SBDs and TBFs made their attacks on Japanese ships, DeBlanc discovered two

Author's Collection

This front view of an F4F-4 shows an unusual aspect of Grumman's tubby little fighter.

more Zeros closing from behind. He engaged and destroyed these two attackers with his badly damaged Wildcat. DeBlanc and a member of his flight, Staff Sergeant James A. Feliton, had to abandon their F4Fs over Kolombangara. A coast-watcher cared for the two Marine aviators until a plane could come from Henderson to retrieve them.

A good closeup of a Wildcat's cockpit and the aircraft's captain on Guadalcanal. Although this F4F displays 19 Japanese flags, it is doubtful that it flew with these since such a large scoreboard would have attracted unwanted attention from the Japanese. Note the reflector gunsight inside the windscreen.

National Archives Photo 80-G-37929

On 31 January 1943, 1stLt Jefferson DeBlanc of VMF-112 earned the Medal of Honor while escorting Marine dive bombers and torpedo-bombers to Vella Gulf. His flight encountered a larger enemy force and during the melee, DeBlanc shot down three float planes and two Zeros before being forced to abandon his own plane at a very low altitude over Japanese-held Kolombangara.

Department of Defense Photo (USMC) 57750

1stLt James E. Swett of VMF-221 was in a flight which rose from Guadalcanal to challenge a large group of enemy planes bent on destroying shipping off the island on 7 April 1943. In a 15-minute period, Swett shot down seven Japanese bombers, a performance which earned him the Medal of Honor.

DeBlanc received the Medal of Honor for his day's work.

The Japanese evacuated Guadalcanal on the night of 7-8 February 1943. The campaign had been costly for both sides, but in the longer term, the Japanese were the big losers. Their myth of invincibility on the ground in the jungle was shattered, as was the myth surrounding the Zero and the pilots who flew it. The lack of reliable records by both sides leaves historians with only wide-ranging estimates of losses. Estimates placed 263 Japanese aircraft lost, while American losses were put at 118. Ninety-four American pilots were also killed in action during the campaign.

Post-Guadalcanal Operations, February-December 1943

Even though the main body of their troops had been evacuated, the Japanese continued to oppose Allied advances by attacking ships and positions. The enemy mounted these attacks through June 1943 from their huge bases in southern Bougainville and from Rabaul on New Britain.

On 7 April 1943, the enemy sent a huge strike against Allied shipping around Guadalcanal. The Japanese force consisted of more than 100 Zero escorts and perhaps 70 bombers, dive bombers, and torpedo bombers. It was an incredibly large raid, the likes of which had not been seen in the Solomons for several months. But it was also, at best, a last desperate gamble by the Japanese in the area.

Henderson scrambled over 100 fighters—Wildcats, Corsairs, P-38s, P-39s, and P-40s. Among this gaggle were the F4Fs of VMF-221. First Lieutenant James E. Swett, leading one of the squadron's divisions, waded into a formation of Val dive bombers. Swett had arrived on Guadalcanal in February and had participated in a few patrols, but had yet to fire his guns in combat.

As he led his four Wildcats toward the Japanese formation, Swett ignored the flak from the American ships below. He targeted two Vals and brought them down. He got a third dive-bomber as a flak shell put a hole in his Wildcat's port wing.

Disengaging, Swett tested his wounded fighter, and satisfied that he could still fly and fight with it, he reentered the fight. Spotting five Vals hightailing it home, he caught up with the little formation and methodically disposed of four of the fixed-gear Vals. The gunner of the fifth bomber, however, hit Swett's Wildcat with a well-aimed burst from his light machine gun, putting .30-caliber ammunition into the Marine fighter's engine and cockpit canopy.

Wounded from the shattering glass, and with his vision obscured from spouting engine oil, Swett pumped more fire into the Val, killing the gunner. The Japanese aircraft disappeared into a cloud, leaving a smoke trail behind. American soldiers later found the Val, with its dead crew. The troops presented Swett with the radio code from the Val's cockpit. However, the aircraft was apparently never credited to Swett's account, leaving his official total for the day at seven.

Swett struggled toward Henderson but over Tulagi harbor, his aircraft's engine quit, leaving him to

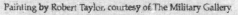

A Marine Wildcat dogfights a Zero over Henderson as other F4Fs finish off another enemy fighter at low level.

Painting by Robert Taylor, courtesy of The Military Gallery

ditch. The Wildcat hit hard, throwing its pilot against the prominent gunsight, stunning him and breaking his nose. Like Joe Foss six months before him, Swett was momentarily trapped as his aircraft sunk, dragging him below the surface. He finally broke free and struggled to the surface where he was rescued by a small picket boat from Gavutu Island. Only one of the four fighters of Swett's division had made it back to Henderson. After intelligence confirmed Swett's incredible one-mission tally, he became the sixth Marine Wildcat pilot to receive the Medal of Honor for action over Guadalcanal.

Swett's engagement was part of the last great aerial battle in the Solomons. The Japanese were forced to turn their attention elsewhere as the American strategy of island-hopping began to gather momentum. All the Marine Corps Wildcat squadrons at Henderson soon transitioned to the next generation of Marine fighter aircraft, the world-beating Vought F4U Corsair which would also provide its own generation of Leatherneck aces in the coming months.

James Swett transitioned to the Corsair and served with VMF-221 when the squadron embarked in the aircraft carrier USS *Bunker Hill* (CV17). By 11 May 1945, when he shot down his last victim, a Japanese kamikaze, he had a total of 15.5 kills in Wildcats and Corsairs.

The Marine Corsair Aces of Bougainville and the Central Pacific, 1943-44

The campaign and victory on Guadalcanal signaled the containment of the seemingly unstoppable Japanese, and the beginning of the long, but ultimately successful, Allied drive through the Pacific to Japan. The first step of the long journey began with the island with the strange name.

Once secured, however, by 7 February 1943, Guadalcanal quickly became the major support base for the remainder of the Solomons campaign. While Marine ground forces slugged their way up the Solomons chain in the middle of 1943, Allied air power provided much-needed support, primarily from newly secured Guadalcanal. Marine and Navy squadrons were accompanied by Army and New Zealand squadrons as they made low-level sweeps along the islands, or escorted bombers against the harbor and airfields around Rabaul. The U.S. Army Air Force sent strikes by B-24 Liberators against Kahili, escorted by Corsairs, P-38s, P-39s, and P-40s. For Marine aviators, it was the time of the Corsair aces.

The First Corsair Ace

Because the Navy decided that the F6F Wildcat was a better carrier fighter than the F4U Vought Corsair, the Marines got a chance to field the first operational squadron to fly the plane. Thus, Major William Gise led the 24 F4U-1s of VMF-124 onto Henderson Field on 12 February 1943.

As the Allied offensive across the Pacific gathered momentum, the fighting above the Solomons and the surrounding islands continued as the Japanese constantly harassed the advancing Allied troops. The Corsair's first engagements were tentative. The pilots of the first squadron, VMF-124, had only an average of 25 hours each in the plane when they landed at Guadalcanal. The very next day, they were off to Bougainvile as escorts for Army B-17s and Navy PB4Y Liberators. It was a lot to ask, but they did it, taking some losses of both

Marine mechanics service an early F4U Corsair, perhaps of VMF-124, on Guadalcanal in early 1943. "Bubbles" is already showing the effects of its harsh tropical environment as well as the constant scuffing of its keepers' boots. Note the Corsair's large gull wings and long nose, which prohibited a clear view forward, especially during taxi and landings.

National Archives 127-N-55431

Enlisting in the Marine Corps in 1933, 1stLt Kenneth A. Walsh eventually went through flight training as a private, gaining his wings in 1937. By 1943, Walsh was in aerial combat over the Solomons and became the first Corsair-mounted ace.

1stLt Ken Walsh of VMF-124 connects his radio lead to his flight helmet before a mission in 1943. He was the first F4U pilot to be decorated with the Medal of Honor, for a mission on 30 August 1943, during which he shot down four Japanese Zeros before ditching his borrowed Corsair.

bombers and escorts. While it was a rough start, the Marines soon settled down and began to exploit the great performance of this new machine, soon to become known to the Japanese as "Whistling Death," and to the Corsair pilots as the "Bent Wing Widow Maker."

After the first few missions, the new experience with the Corsair's capabilities began to really take hold. First Lieutenant Kenneth A. Walsh, a former enlisted pilot (he received his wings of gold as a *private*), shot down three enemy aircraft on 1 April. Six weeks later, after several patrols, Walsh dropped three more Zeros on 13 May 1943, becoming the first Corsair ace. By 15 August, Walsh had 10 victories to his credit.

On 30 August, he was scheduled to fly escort for Army B-24s on a strike against the Japanese airfield at Kahili, Bougainville. Walsh's four-plane section launched before noontime to make the flight to a forward base on Banika in the Russell Islands. After refueling and

grabbing some lunch, the four Marine pilots took off again to rendezvous with the bombers. As the escorts—more F4Us and Army P-38s—joined up with the bombers, Walsh's engine acted up, forcing him to make an emergency landing at Munda.

A friend, Major James L. Neefus, was in charge of the Munda airfield, and he let Walsh choose another fighter from Corsairs that were parked on Munda's airstrip. Walsh took off in his borrowed fighter and headed toward Kahili to try to find and rejoin with his division. As he finally approached the enemy base, he saw the B-24s in their bomb runs, beset by swarms of angry Zeros. Alone, at least for the moment, Walsh piled into the enemy interceptors which had already begun to work on the Army bombers.

As Walsh fought off several attacks by some 50 Zeros, thereby disrupting to a degree their attack on the bombers, he wondered where all the other American fighters might be. Finally, several other Corsairs appeared to relieve the hard-pressed ace. As other aircraft took the burden from Walsh, he eased his damaged fighter east to take stock of his situation. He was able to shoot down two Zeros, but the enemy interceptors were nearly overwhelming. The B-24s were struggling to turn for home as more Zeros took off from Kahili.

Lieutenant Walsh managed to down two more Zeros before he had to disengage his badly damaged Corsair. Pursued by the Japanese, who pumped cannon and machine gun fire into his plane, Walsh knew he would not return this Corsair to

This VMF-124 F4U-1, No.13, was flown by 1stLt Ken Walsh during his first combat tour in which he became the first Corsair-mounted ace.

Major Neefus at Munda. Several Corsairs and a lone P-40 arrived to scatter the Zeros which were using Walsh for target practice.

He ditched his battered fighter off Vella Lavella and was picked up by the Seabees who borrowed a boat after watching the Marine Corsair splash into the sea. For his spirited single-handed defense of the B-24s over Bougainville, Lieutenant Walsh became the first Cor-

Maj Gregory "Pappy" Boyington became the best known Marine ace. A member of the Flying Tigers in China before World War II, he later commanded VMF-122 before taking over VMF-214. By early January 1944, he was the Corps' leading scorer. Here, the colorful Boyington, center, relaxes with some of his pilots.

sair pilot to receive the Medal of Honor. The four Zeros he shot down during this incredible mission ran his score to 20.

Ken Walsh shot down one more aircraft, another Zero, off Okinawa on 22 June 1945, the day the island was secured. At the time, Walsh was the operations officer for VMF-222, shorebased on the newly secured island.

A series of assaults during the spring and summer of 1943 netted the Allies several important islands up the Solomons chain. An amphibious assault of Bougainville at Empress Augusta Bay on 1 November 1943, caught the Japanese defenders off guard. In spite of Japanese reaction and reinforcement, a secure perimeter was quickly established, and within 40 days, the first of three airfields was in operation with two more to follow by the new year. Aircraft from these strips flew fighter sweeps first, later to be followed by daily escorted SBD and TBF strikes. With the establishment of this air strength at Bougainville, the rest of the island was effectively bypassed, and the fate of Rabaul sealed.

Marine aircraft began flying from their base at Torokina Point at Empress Augusta Bay, the site for the initial landing on Bougainville's midwestern coast. Navy Seabees then quickly hacked out two more airstrips from the jungle—Piva North and Piva South. Piva Village was a settlement on the Piva River, east of the airfield complex.

The official Marine Corps history noted that "whenever there was no combat air patrol over the beachhead, the Japanese were quite apt to drop shells into the airfield area. The Seabees and Marine engineers moved to the end of the field which was not being hit and continued to work."

Comparative Table for Main Types of Fighters

Aircraft	Length	Span	Engine (hp)	Max Speed (mph)/ altitude (feet)	Range normal/max (miles)	Armament	Number Built
U.S. Navy							
F4F-4 Wildcat	28'9"	38'0"	Pratt & Whitney R-1 830-86 (1,200)	320/19,400	910/1,250	4x (later 6) .50-cal. machine guns	1,168
4U-1 Corsair	33'4"	41'0"	Pratt & Whitney R-2800-8 (2,000)	417/ 19,900	1,015/1,562	6x.50-cal. machine guns	9,444[1]
USAAF							
P-400 (P-39D) Airacobra	30'2"	34'0"	Allison V-1710 (1,150)	335/ 5,000	600/1,100	1x20mm can. 4x.30-cal. 2x.50-cal. machine guns	179[2]
P-40E Warhawk	31'2"	37'4"	Allison V-1710 (1,150)	335/ 5,000	650/ 850	6x.50-cal. machine guns	2,320
Japanese Navy							
A6M2 Model 21 Zero-sen Zeke)	29'8"	39'4"	Nakajima Sakai 12 (925)	331/ 15,000	1,160/ 1,930	2x20mm can. 2x7.7mm machine guns	1,100[3]
A6M2-N (Rufe)	33'1"	39'4"	Nakajima Sakai 12 (925)	270/ 16,400	714/ 1,107	2x20mm can. 2x7.7mm machine guns	327
Japanese Army							
Ki.43-1a Hayabusa (Oscar)	28'11"	37'6"	Nakajima Ha-25 (950)	308/ 13,100	745 max	2x7.7mm or 12.7mm machine guns	716
Ki.61-1a Hien (Tony)	28'8"	39'4"	Kawasaki Ha-40 (1,175)	368/ 16,000	373/ 684	2x12.7mm 2x7.7mm machine guns	1,380

[1] Includes all variants of the F4U-1, i.e., the -1, -1A, -1C (armed with 4x20mm cannon), and -1D, as well as those built by Goodyear as the FG-1A/D, and by Brewster as the F3A-1D.

[2] The amount reclaimed by the USAAF from the original RAF order of 675. Approximately 100 P-400 and 90 P-39Ds served with the USAAF in the Pacific. Others served with the Soviet Air Force, and the USAAF in the Middle East and the Mediterranean theater.

[3] Production numbers for many Japanese aircraft are difficult to pin down. The best estimate places A6M2 production at over 1,100.

Major Gregory "Pappy" Boyington

The One and Only 'Pappy'

Every one of the Corps' aces had special qualities that set him apart from his squadron mates. Flying and shooting skills, tenacity, aggressiveness, and a generous share of luck—the aces had these in abundance. One man probably had more than his share of these qualities, and that was the legendary "Pappy" Boyington.

A native of Idaho, Gregory Boyington went through flight training as a Marine Aviation Cadet, earning a reputation for irreverence and high jinks that did not go down well with his superiors. His thirst for adventure, as well as his accumulated financial debts, led him to resign his commission as a first lieutenant and join the American Volunteer Group (AVG), better known as the Flying Tigers. Like other service pilots who joined the AVG, he first resigned his commission and this letter was then put in a safe to be redeemed and torn up when he rejoined the Marine Corps.

Boyington claimed to have shot down six Japanese aircraft while with the Flying Tigers. However, AVG records were poorly kept, and were lost in air raids. To compound the problem, the U.S. Air Force does not officially recognize the kills made by the AVG, even though the Tigers were eventually absorbed into the Fourteenth Air Force, led by Major General Claire Chennault. Thus, the best confirmation that can be obtained on Boyington's record with the AVG is that he scored 3.5 kills.

Whatever today's accounts show, Boyington returned to the U.S. claiming to be one of America's first aces. He was perhaps the first Marine aviator to have flown in combat against the Japanese, though, and he felt he would easily regain his commission in the Marine Corps. To his frustration, no one in any service seemed to want him. His reputation was well known and this made his reception not exactly open armed.

Boyington finally telegrammed his qualifications to Secretary of the Navy Frank Knox, and as a result, found himself back in the Marine Corps on active duty as a Reserve major. He deployed as executive officer of VMF-122 from the West Coast to the Solomons. He was based at Espiritu Santo, initially flying squadron training, non-combat missions. He deployed for a short but inactive tour at Guadalcanal in March 1943, and after the squadron was withdrawn, he relieved Major Elmer Brackett as commanding officer in April 1943. His first command tour was disappointing. He eventually landed in VMF-112, which he commanded for three weeks in the rear area. Prior to forward deployment, he broke his leg while wrestling and was hospitalized.

Boyington got another chance and took command of a reconstituted VMF-214. The original unit had returned from a combat tour, during which it had lost its commanding officer, Major William Pace. When the squadron returned from a short rest and recreation tour in Australia, the decision was made to reorganize the unit because the squadron did not have a full complement of combat-ready pilots. Thus, the squadron number went to a newly organized squadron under Major Boyington. In his illuminating wartime memoir, *Once They*

Black Sheep pilots scramble toward their F4U-1 "birdcage" Corsairs. The early model fighters had framed cockpit canopies. The next F4U-1As and subsequent models used bubble canopies which enhanced the limited visibility from the fighter's cockpit.

Were Eagles: The Men of the Black Sheep Squadron, the squadron intelligence officer, First Lieutenant Frank Walton, described how Boyington got the new squadron command:

Major Boyington was the right rank for a squadron commander; he was an experienced combat pilot; he was available; and the need was great. These assets overcame such reservations as the general [Major General Ralph J. Mitchell, Wing Commander of the 1st Marine Aircraft Wing] may have had about his personal problems. General [Mitchell] made the decision. "We need an aggressive combat leader. We'll go with Boyington." The squadron had its commander.

Much has been written about Boyington and his squadron. At 31, Boyington was older than his 22-year-old lieutenants. His men called him "Gramps" or "Pappy." In prewar days, he was called "Rats," after the Russian-born actor, Gregory Ratoff. The squadron wanted to call themselves the alliterative "Boyington's Bastards," but 1940s sensitivities would not allow such language. They decided on the more evocative "Black Sheep."

The popular image of VMF-214 as a collection of malcontents and ne'er-do-wells is not at all accurate. The television program of the late 1970s did nothing to dispel this inaccurate impression. In truth, Pappy's squadron was much like any other fighter squadron, with a cross-section of people of varying capabilities and experience. The two things that welded the new squadron into such a fearsome fighting unit was its new mount, the F4U-1 Corsair, and its indomitable leader.

Boyington took his squadron to Munda on New Georgia in Septem-

Author's Collection

Pappy briefs his pilots before a mission from Espiritu Santo. Front row, from left: Boyington, holding paper, Stanley R. Bailey, Virgil G. Ray, Robert A. Alexander; standing, from left: William N. Case, Rolland N. Rinabarger, Don H. Fisher, Henry M. Bourgeois, John F. Begert, Robert T. Ewing, Denmark Groover, Jr., Burney L. Tucker.

ber. On the 16th, the Black Sheep flew their first mission, a bomber escort to Ballale, a Japanese airfield on a small island about five miles southeast of Bougainville. The mission turned into a free-for-all as about 40 Zeros descended on the bombers. Boyington downed a Zero for his squadron's first kill. He quickly added four more. Six other Black Sheep scored kills. It was an auspicious debut, marred only by the loss of one -214 pilot, Captain Robert T. Ewing.

The following weeks were filled with continuous action. Boyington and his squadron rampaged through the enemy formations, whether the Marine Corsairs were escorting bombers, or making pure fighter sweeps. The frustrated Japanese tried to lure Pappy into several traps, but the pugnacious ace taunted them over the radio, chal-

Maintenance crews service this F4U-1 at a Pacific base. The Corsair's size is shown to advantage in this view, as is the bubble canopy of the late-production -1s and subsequent models.

Author's Collection

lenging them to come and get him.

By mid-December 1943, VMF-214, along with the other Allied fighter squadrons, began mounting large fighter sweeps staged through the new fighter strip at Torokina Point on Bougainville. Author Barrett Tillman described the state of affairs in the area at the end of December 1943:

...Boyington and other senior airmen saw the disadvantage of [these] large fighter sweeps. They intimidated the opposition into remaining grounded, which was the opposite reaction desired. A set of guidelines was drawn up for future operations. It specified that the maximum number of fighters should be limited to

no more than 48. As few aircraft types and squadrons should be employed as possible, for better coordination and mutual support.

This strategy was fine, except that Boyington was beginning to feel the pressure that being a top ace seemed to bring. People kept wondering when Pappy would achieve, then break, the magic number of 26, Captain Eddie Rickenbacker's score in World War I. Joe Foss had already equalled the early ace's total, but was now out of action. Boyington scored four kills on 23 December 1943, bringing his tally to 24. Boyington was certainly feeling the pressure to break Rickenbacker's 25-year-old record. Boyington's intelligence officer, First

Lieutenant Frank Walton, wrote of his tenseness and quick flareups when pressed about when and by how much he would surpass the magic 26.

A few days before his final mission, Boyington reacted to a persistent public affairs officer. "Sure, I'd like to break the record," said Boyington. "Who wouldn't? I'd like to get 40 if I could. The more we can shoot down here, the fewer there'll be up the line to stop us."

Later that night, Boyington told Walton, "Christ, I don't care if I break the record or not, if they'd just leave me alone." Walton told his skipper the squadron was behind him and that he was probably in the best position he'd ever be in to break the record.

The fighter strip at Torokina was hacked out of the Bougainville jungle. This December 1943 view shows a lineup of Corsairs and   *an SBD, which is completing its landing rollout past a grading machine still working to finish the new landing field.*

1stLt Robert M. Hanson of VMF-215 enjoyed a brief career in which he shot down 20 of his final total of 25 Japanese planes in 13 days. He was shot down during a strafing run on 3 February, 1944, a day before his 24th birthday.

"You'll never have another chance," Walton said. "It's now or never."

"Yes," Boyington agreed, "I guess you're right."

Like a melodrama, however, Boyington's life now seemed to revolve around raising his score. Even those devoted members of his squadron could not help wondering—if only to cheer their squadron commander on—when he would do it.

Pappy's agony was about to come to a crashing halt. He got a single kill on 27 December during a huge fight against 60 Zeros. But, after taking off on a mission against Rabaul on 2 January 1944, at the head of 56 Navy and Marine fighters, Boyington had problems with his Corsair's engine. He returned without adding to his score.

The following day, he launched at the head of another sweep staging through Bougainville. By late morning, other VMF-214 pilots returned with the news that Boyington had, indeed, been in action. When they last saw him, Pappy had

already disposed of one Zero, and together with his wingman, Captain George M. Ashmun, was hot on the tails of other victims.

The initial happy anticipation turned to apprehension as the day wore on and neither Pappy nor Ashmun returned. By the afternoon, without word from other bases, the squadron had to face the unthinkable: Boyington was missing. The Black Sheep mounted patrols to look for their leader, but within a few days, they had to admit that Pappy was not coming back.

In fact, Boyington and his wingman had been shot down after Pappy had bagged three more Zeros, thus bringing his claimed total to 28, breaking the Rickenbacker tally, and establishing Boyington as the top-scoring Marine ace of the war, and, for that matter, of all time. However, these final victories were unknown until Boyington's return from a Japanese prison camp in 1945. Boyington's last two kills were thus unconfirmed. The only one who could

One of Boyington's Black Sheep, 1stLt John F. Bolt, already an ace, shot down his sixth plane over Rabaul in early January 1944. During the Korean war, when he was flying as an exchange pilot with the Air Force, he shot down six North Korean planes to become the Marine Corps' first jet ace.

Capt Donald N. Aldrich was a 20-kill ace with VMF-215, and had learned to fly with the Royal Canadian Air Force before the U.S. entered the war. Although he survived the war, he was killed in a flying mishap in 1947.

have seen Pappy's victories was his wingman, Captain Ashmun, shot down along with his skipper. While there is no reason to doubt his claims, the strict rules of verifying kills were apparently relaxed for the returning hero when he was recovered from a prisoner of war camp after the war.

Pappy and his wingman had been overwhelmed by a swarm of Zeros and had to bail out of their faltering Corsairs near Cape St. George on New Ireland. Captain Ashmun was never recovered, but Boyington was retrieved by a Japanese submarine after being strafed by the vengeful Zeros that had just shot him down. Boyington spent the next 20 months as a prisoner of war, although no one in the U.S. knew it until after V-J Day.

He endured torture and beatings during interrogations, and was finally rescued when someone painted "Boyington Here!" on the roof of his prison barracks. Aircraft dropping supplies to the prisoners shortly after the ceasefire in August 1945 spotted the message and soon

Three of the Corps' top aces pose at Torokina in early 1944. From left: 1stLt Robert Hanson, Capt Donald N. Aldrich, and Capt Harold Spears were members of VMF-215 during the busy period following the loss of Pappy Boyington. The three aviators accounted for a combined total of 60 Japanese aircraft.

Capt Harold L. Spears was Robert Hanson's flight leader on the day Hanson was shot down and killed after Spears gave Hanson permission to make a strafing run against a Japanese position in December 1944.

On 30 June 1943, 1stLt Wilbur J. Thomas of VMF-213 shot down four enemy planes while providing air cover for American operations on New Georgia. Two weeks later, on 15 July, he shot down three more Japanese bombers. Before he left the Pacific, his total of kills was 18½.

everyone knew that Pappy was coming back.

Although he had never received a single decoration while he was in combat, Boyington returned to the U.S. to find that he not only had been awarded the Navy Cross, but the Medal of Honor as well, albeit "posthumously."

With Pappy Boyington gone, several other young Marine aviators began to make themselves known. The most productive, and unfortunately, the one with the shortest career, was First Lieutenant Robert M. Hanson of VMF-215. Although born in India of missionary parents, Hanson called Massachusetts home. A husky, competitive man, he quickly took to the life of a Marine combat aviator.

During his first and second tours, flying from Vella Lavella with other squadrons, including Boyington's Black Sheep, Hanson shot down five Japanese planes, although during one of these fights, he, himself,

was forced to ditch his Corsair in Empress Augusta Bay.

For his third tour, he joined VMF-215 at Torokina. By mid-January, Hanson had begun such a hot streak of kills, that the young pilot had earned the name "Butcher Bob." Hanson shot Japanese planes down in bunches. On 18 January 1944, he disposed of five enemy aircraft. On 24 January, he added four more Zeros. Another four Japanese planes went down before Hanson's Corsair on 30 January. His score now stood at 25, 20 of which had been gained in 13 days in only six missions. Hanson's successes were happening so quickly that he was relatively unknown outside his combat area. Very few combat correspondents knew of his record until later.

Lieutenant Hanson took off for a mission on 3 February 1944. The next day would be his 24th birthday, and the squadron's third tour would end in a few days. He was going back home. He called his

flight commander, Captain Harold L. Spears, and asked if he could strafe Japanese antiaircraft artillery positions at Cape St. George on New Ireland, the same general area over which Pappy Boyington had been shot down a month before.

Hanson made his run, firing his plane's six .50-caliber machine guns. The Japanese returned fire as the big, blue-gray Marine fighter rocketed past, seemingly under control. However, Hanson's plane dove into the water from a low altitude, leaving only an oil slick.

Hanson's meteoric career saw him become the highest-scoring Marine Corsair ace, and the second Marine high-scorer, one behind Joe Foss. Lieutenant Hanson received a posthumous Medal of Honor for his third tour of combat. As Barrett Tillman points out in his book on the F4U, Hanson "became the third and last Corsair pilot to receive the Medal of Honor in World War II. And the youngest."

Japanese Pilots in the Solomons Air War

The stereotypical picture of a small, emaciated Japanese pilot, wearing glasses whose lenses were the thickness of the bottoms of Coke bottles, grasping the stick of his bamboo-and-rice-paper airplane (the design was probably stolen from the U.S., too) did not persist for long after the war began. The first American aircrews to return from combat knew that they had faced some of the world's most experienced combat pilots equipped with some pretty impressive airplanes.

Author's Collection.

A rebuilt late-model Zero shows off the clean lines of the A6M series, which changed little during the production run of more than 10,000 fighters.

Author's Collection

Newly commissioned Ens Junichi Sasai in May 1941.

Certainly, Japanese society was completely alien to most Americans. Adherence to ancestral codes of honor and a national history—one of constant internal, localized strife where personal weakness was not tolerated, especially in the Samurai class of professional warriors—did not permit the individual Japanese soldier to surrender even in the face of overwhelming odds.

This capability did not come by accident. Japanese training was tough. In some respects, it went far beyond the legendary limits of even U.S. Marine Corps boot training. However, as the war turned against them, the Japanese relaxed their stringent prewar requirements and mass-produced pilots to replace the veterans who were lost at Midway and in the Solomons. For instance, before the war, pilots learned navigation and how to pack a parachute. After 1942, these subjects were eliminated from training to save time.

Young men who were accepted for flight training were subjected to an excruciating preflight indoctrination into military life. Their instructors—mostly enlisted—were literally their rulers, with nearly life-or-

death control of the recruits' existence. After surviving the physical training, the recruits began flight training where the rigors of their preflight classes were maintained. By the time Japanese troops evacuated Guadalcanal in February 1943, however, their edge had begun wearing thin as they had lost many of their most experienced pilots and flight commanders, along with their aircraft.

The failed Japanese adventure at Midway in June 1942, as well as the heavy losses in the almost daily combat over Guadalcanal and the Solomons deprived them of irreplaceable talent. Even the most experienced pilots eventually came up against a losing roll of the dice.

As noted in the main text, Japanese aces such as Sakai, Sasai, and Ota were invalided out of combat, or eventually killed. Rotation of pilots out of the war zone was a system employed neither by the Japanese nor the Germans, as a matter of fact. As several surviving Axis aces have noted in their memoirs, they flew until they couldn't. Indeed many Japanese and German aces flew until 1945—if they were lucky enough to survive—accumulating incredible numbers of sorties and combat hours, as well as high scores which doubled and tripled the final tallies of their American counterparts.

Unfortunately, Japanese records are not as complete as Allied histories, perhaps because of the tremendous damage and confusion wrought by the U.S. strategic bombing during the last year of the war. Thus, certainly Japanese scores are not as firm as they are for Allied aviators.

In the popularly accepted sense, the Japanese did not have "aces." Those pilots who achieved high scores were referred to as Gekitsui-O (Shoot-Down Kings). A pilot's report of his successes was taken at face value, without a confirmation system such as required by the Allies. Without medals or formal recognition, it was believed that there was little need for self-promotion. Fighters did not have gun cameras, either. Japanese air strategy was to inflict as much damage as possible without worrying about confirming a kill. (This outwardly cavalier attitude about claiming victories is somewhat suspect since many Zeros carried large "scoreboards" on their tails and fuselages. These markings might have been attributed to the aircraft rather than to a specific pilot.)

Enlisted pilots of the Tainan Kokutai pose at Rabaul in 1942. Several of these aviators would be among the top Japanese aces, including Saburo Sakai (middle row, second from left), and Hiroyoshi Nishizawa (standing, first on left).

A lineup of A6M2 Zeros at Buin in 1943. By this time, the heavy combat over Guadalcanal had been replaced by engagements with Marine Corsairs over the approaches to Bougainville. Japanese Navy aircraft occasionally flew from land bases, as these Zeros, although they are actually assigned to the carrier Zuikaku.

The Aces

Although the men in the Zeros were probably much like—at least in temperament—Marine Wildcat and Corsair pilots they opposed, the Imperial Japanese Navy pilots had an advantage: many of them had been flying combat for perhaps a year—maybe longer—before meeting the untried American aviators over Guadalcanal in August 1942. Saburo Sakai was severely wounded during an engagement with U.S. Navy SBDs on the opening day of the invasion. He re-

turned to Japan with about 60 kills to his credit. Actually, because he was so badly wounded early in the Guadalcanal fighting, Sakai never got a chance to engage Marine Corps pilots. They were still in transit to the Solomons two weeks after Sakai had been invalided home. (His commonly accepted final score of 64 is only a best guess, even by his own logbook.)

After graduating from flight training, Sakai joined a squadron in China flying Mitsubishi Type 96 fighters, small, open-cockpit, fixed-landing-gear fighters. As a third-class petty officer, Sakai shot down a Russian-built SB-3 bomber in October 1939. He later joined the Tainan Kokutai (Tainan air wing), which would become one of the Navy's premier fighter units, and participated in the Pacific war's opening actions in the Philippines.

A colorful personality, Sakai was also a dedicated flight leader. He never lost a wingman in combat, and also tried to pass on his hard-won expertise to more junior pilots. After a particularly unsuccessful mission in April 1942, where his flight failed to bring down a single American bomber from a flight of seven Martin B-26 Marauders, he sternly lectured his pilots about maintaining flight discipline instead of hurling themselves against their foes. His words had great effect—Sakai was respected by subordinates and superiors alike—and his men soon formed a well-working unit, responsible for many kills in the early months of the Pacific war.

Typically, Junichi Sasai, a lieutenant, junior grade, and one of Sakai's young aces with 27 confirmed kills, was posthumously promoted two grades to lieutenant commander. This practice was common for those

Japanese aviators with proven records, or high scores, who were killed during the war. Japan was unique among all the combatants during the war in that it had no regular or defined system of awards, except for occasional inclusion in war news—what the British might call being "mentioned in dispatches."

This somewhat frustrating lack of recognition was described by Masatake Okumiya, a Navy fighter commander, in his classic book *Zero!* (with Jiro Horikoshi). Describing a meeting with senior officers, he asked them, "Why in the name of heaven does Headquarters delay so long in according our combat men the honors they deserve?...Our Navy does absolutely nothing to recognize its heroes...."

LCdr Tadashi Nakajima, who led the Tainan Air Group, was typical of the more senior aviators. His responsibilities were largely administrative but he tried to fly missions whenever his schedule permitted, usually with unproductive results. He led several of the early missions over Guadalcanal and survived to lead a Shiden unit in 1944. It is doubtful that Nakajima scored more than 2 or 3 kills.

Lt (j.g.) Junichi Sadai of the Tainan Air Group. This 1942 photo shows the young combat leader, of such men as Sakai and Nishizawa, shortly before his death over Guadalcanal.

Occasionally, senior officers would give gifts, such as ceremonial swords, to those pilots who had performed great services. And sometimes, superiors would try to buck the unbending system without much success. Saburo Sakai described one instance in June 1942 where the captain in charge of his wing summoned him and Lieutenant Sasai to his quarters.

Dejectedly, the captain told his two pilots how he had asked Tokyo to recognize them for their great accomplishments. "...Tokyo is adamant about making any changes at this time," he said. "They have refused even

to award a medal or to promote in rank." The captain's deputy commander then said how the captain had asked that Sasai be promoted to commander—an incredible jump of three grades—and that Sakai be commissioned as an ensign.

Perhaps one of the most enigmatic, yet enduring, personalities of the Zero pilots was the man who is generally acknowledged to be the top-scoring Japanese ace, Hiroyoshi Nishizawa. Saburo Sakai described him as "tall and lanky for a Japanese, nearly five feet, eight inches in height," and possessing "almost supernatural vision."

These A6M3s are from the Tainan Air Group, and several sources have identified aircraft 106 as being flown by top ace Nishizawa. Typically, these fighters carry a single centerline fuel tank. The Zero's range was phenomenal, sometimes extending to nearly 1,600 miles, making for a very long flight for its exhausted pilots.

Petty Officer Hiroyoshi Nishizawa at Lae, New Guinea, in 1942. Usually considered the top Japanese ace, Navy or Army. A definitive total will probably never be determined. Nishizawa died while flying as a passenger in a transport headed for the Philippines in October 1944. The transport was caught by American Navy Hellcats, and Lt(j.g.) Harold Newell shot it down.

Petty Officer Sadamu Komachi flew throughout the Pacific War, from Pearl Harbor to the Solomons, from Bougainville to the defense of the Home Islands. His final score was 18.

Nishizawa kept himself usually aloof, enjoying a detached but respected status as he rolled up an impressive victory tally through the Solomons campaign. He was eventually promoted to warrant officer in November 1943. Like a few other high-scoring aces, Nishizawa met death in an unexpected manner in the Philippines. He was shot down while riding as a passenger in a bomber used to transport him to another base to ferry a Zero in late October 1944. In keeping with the established tradition, Nishizawa was posthumously promoted two ranks to lieutenant junior grade. His score has been variously given as 102, 103, and as high as 150. However, the currently accepted total for him is 87.

Henry Sakaida, a well-known authority on Japanese pilots in World War II, wrote:

No Japanese pilot ever scored more than 100 victories! In fact, Nishizawa entered combat in 1942 and his period of active duty was around 18 months. On the other hand, Lieutenant junior grade Tetsuo Iwamoto fought from 1938 until the end of the war. If there is a top Navy ace, it's him.

Iwamoto claimed 202 victories, many of which were against U.S. Marine Corps aircraft, including 142 at Rabaul. I don't believe his claims are accurate, but I don't believe Nishizawa's total of 87, either. (I might believe 30.) Among Iwamoto's claims were 48 Corsairs and 48 SBDs! His actual score might be around 80.

Several of Sho-ichi Sugita's kills—which are informally reckoned to total 70—were Marine aircraft. He was barely 19 when he first saw combat in the Solomons. (He had flown at Midway but saw little of the fighting.) Flying from Buin on the southern tip of Bougainville, he first scored on 1 December 1942, against a USAAF B-17. Sugita was one of the six Zero escort pilots that watched as P-38s shot down Admiral Yamamoto's Betty on 18 April 1943. There was little they could do to alert the bombers carrying the admiral and his staff since their Zeros' primitive radios had been taken out to save weight.

The problem of keeping accurate records probably came from the directive issued in June 1943 by Tokyo forbidding the recording of individual records, the better to foster teamwork in the seemingly once-invincible Zero squadrons. Prior to the directive, Japanese Zero pilots were the epitome of the hunter-pilots personified by the World War I German ace, Baron Manfred von Richthofen. The Japanese Navy pilots roamed where they wished and attacked when they wanted, assured in the superiority of their fighters.

Occasionally, discipline would disappear as flight leaders dove into Allied bomber formations, their wingmen hugging their tails as they attacked with their maneuverable Zeros, seemingly simulating their Samurai role models whose expertise with swords is legendary.

Most of the Japanese aces, and most of the rank-and-file pilots, were enlisted petty officers. In fact, no other combatant nation had so many enlisted fighter pilots. The U.S. Navy and Marine Corps had a relatively few enlisted pilots who flew in combat in World War II and for a short time in Korea. Britain and Germany had a considerable number of enlisted aviators without whose services they could not have maintained the momentum of their respective campaigns.

However, the Japanese officer corps was relatively small, and the number of those commissioned pilots serving as combat flight commanders was even smaller. Thus, the main task of fighting the growing Allied air threat in the Pacific fell to dedicated enlisted pilots, many of them barely out of their teens.

During a recent interview, Saburo Sakai shed light on the role of Japanese officer-pilots. He said:

They did fight, but generally, they were not very good because they were inexperienced. In my group, it would be the enlisted pilots that would first spot the enemy. The first one to see the enemy would lead and signal the others to follow. And the officer pilot would be back there, wondering where everyone went! In this sense, it was the enlisted pilots who led, not the officers.

Department of Defense Photo (USMC) 47912

Maj Edward Overend, shown here in a Wildcat in San Diego in 1945, flew with the Flying Tigers, shooting down five Japanese aircraft, thus becoming one of the first American aces of the Pacific war, albeit under another country's colors. Maj Overend scored 3.5 kills while leading VMF-321, for a combined total of 8.5 victories in P-40Bs and F4U-1As.

Other Marine Aces

Although the colorful time of the Solomons Campaign, and the equally colorful men like Boyington and Hanson, were gone, other Leatherneck aviators achieved sizeable scores, and a measure of fame, if only within their operating areas and squadrons.

VMF-214's five-month tour of combat created eight aces, including Pappy Boyington. The Black Sheep accounted for 97 Japanese aircraft downed. VMF-215's tour lasted four-and-a-half months, and Bob Hanson and his squadron mates—the squadron's roster included 10 aces—destroyed 137 enemy aircraft, 106 in the last six weeks.

Besides Boyington, the Black Sheep alumnus who had one of the most interesting careers was John Bolt. Then-First Lieutenant Bolt shot down six aircraft in the Pacific. Ten years later, now-Major Bolt flew F-86s as an exchange pilot with the U.S. Air Force in Korea. During a three-month period, May-July 1953, he shot down six Russian-built MiG-15s, becoming the Marine Corps' first and only jet ace, and one of a very select number of pilots who became aces in two wars.

While Lieutenant Robert Hanson was the star of VMF-215 for a few short weeks, there were two captains who were just as busy. Donald N. Aldrich eventually scored 20 kills, while Harold L. Spears accounted for 15 Japanese planes. The two aces were among the senior flight leaders of VMF-215.

Don Aldrich had been turned down by recruiters before Pearl Harbor because he was married. Like many other eager young men of his generation, he went across the Canadian border and enlisted in the Royal Canadian Air Force in February 1941. He got his wings that November. But the RCAF put the new aviator to work as an instructor. When the U.S. entered the war, Aldrich had no trouble rejoining his countrymen, and eventually got his wings of gold as a Marine aviator, following which, he headed for the Solomons. From August 1943 to February 1944, in three combat tours, Captain Aldrich gained an impressive number of kills, 20. Although he survived the war, he died in an operational accident in 1947.

Harold Spears was commissioned a Marine second lieutenant and got his Marine commission and his wings in August 1942. He joined VMF-215 as the squadron wandered around the various forward bases near Bougainville. Spears wanted to make the service his career, and shortly after finishing his combat tour, during which he shot down 15 Japanese planes, he was assigned to El Toro, and eventually to a new fighter squadron, VMF-462.

One of the most successful but least known Marine Corsair aces was First Lieutenant Wilbur J. Thomas, whom Barrett Tillman called "one of the deadliest fighter pilots the Corps ever produced." He scored 18.5 kills while flying with VMF-213. Thomas' combat career is remarkable because he scored most of his kills in a one-month period during the hotly contested landings on Rendova and Vangunu islands in mid-1944.

After staying in the rear area of the New Hebrides, Thomas was finally transferred to the combat zone. He flew his first missions in June and July 1943. His mission on 30 June was a CAP mission over amphibious landings at Wickham Anchorage on the southern tip of New Georgia.

Zero fighter-bombers prepare to launch for a raid from their Bougainville base in late 1943. Originally an air superiority weapon, the Zero toted light bombs as required, and ended the war as one of the primary aircraft used by the Kamikaze suicide pilots.

Fifteen Zeros pounced Thomas's fighters. After he had become separated from his group, seven Zeros had attacked the lone F4U, but, undeterred by the odds, Thomas turned into the Japanese, eventually shooting down four of them. He was awarded the Distinguished Flying Cross for this mission. Three weeks later, on 17 July, Thomas and his wingman attacked a group of Japanese bombers and their Zero escort, and shot down one of the bombers.

Thomas was on the receiving end of enemy fire on 23 September. After shooting down three Zeros, and splitting a fourth with his wingman, the young ace found he had taken hits in the oil lines. His engine seized and he glided toward the water, eventually bailing out at 3,000 feet. He scrambled into his rubber raft and waited for rescue. He paddled for five hours to keep from drifting to enemy positions. After 10 hours, a Consolidated Catalina flying boat (PBY) set down beside him and brought him home.

By the time VMF-213 left for the States in December, Wilbur Thomas had scored 16.5 kills in five dogfights. He returned for another combat tour, this time on board the carrier *Essex* (CV 9) headed for the South China Sea and Japanese bases in Southeast Asia. He added two more kills to his previous score when he took out two Zeros near Tokyo during *Essex's* first strike against the Japanese Home Islands on the afternoon of 16 February 1945.

Again, as did several of the young aces who managed to survive the war, now-Captain Thomas died in a postwar flying mishap in 1947.

By mid-1944, the war had moved on, past the Solomons and Bougainville, closer to Japan and into the final battles in the Philippines and on to Iwo Jima and Okinawa. There were still occasional encounters in these now-rear areas until the end of the war, and other Marine aviators became aces, but the end of the Solomons Campaign also saw the end of the heyday of the aces.

Fighter pilots and their missions sometimes fall into a nondescript category. By themselves, they rarely decide the outcome of major battles or campaigns, although exceptions might well be Guadalcanal and the Battle of Britain.

The Cactus fighters defended their base daily against enemy raids, and the Marine Corps aces were colorful. They established a tradition of dedication, courage, and skill for their successors in future generations of military aviators. It is 50 years since John Smith, Bob Galer, Marion Carl, Joe Foss, and Greg Boyington led their squadrons into the swirling dogfights over the Solomons. But the legacy these early Marine aces left to their modern successors lives on in a new era of advanced weapons and technology.

Maj Robert Galer with his ubiquitous baseball cap leans against his Wildcat. "Barbara Jane" was a high school sweetheart. (He didn't marry her.) The square panel directly beneath the aircraft's wing was an observational window.

Photo courtesy of BGen Robert Galer, USMC (Ret)

Researching the Aces' Scores

Meticulous investigation by Dr. Frank Olynyk has refined and changed the established list of aces. In most respects, he has reduced by one or two kills an individual's score, but in some instances, he has generated enough doubt about the vital fifth kill that at least two aviators have lost their status as aces during World War II. One man, Technical Sergeant John W. Andre of night-fighter squadron VMF(N)-541, shot down four Japanese planes in the Pacific, and scored a fifth kill in Korea. Thus, he is a bonafide ace, but not solely by his service in World War II.

In an article published in the Summer 1981 issue of *Fortitudine*, the bulletin of the Marine Corps History and Museums Division, Dr.

Olynyk discussed the problems associated with compiling records of aerial kills, especially for the Marine Corps. Whether an enemy aircraft which was last seen descending with a trail of smoke should be considered destroyed cannot always be decided. Thus, several "smokers" were claimed as definite kills.

He also commented, "...most of the pilots whose scores are subject to some uncertainty are all from the 1942-early 1943 period when air combat was the heaviest. War diaries from this period are often incomplete, or even non-existent..."

Retired Brigadier General Robert Galer put the question of aces and their kills in perspective. In a recent letter to the author he wrote, "Aces' scores are not an exact number. There were too many people

shooting at the same targets. The enemy might sustain some battle damage, such as in the engine, but they could run for another five minutes. It was tough to be accurate."

Then-Captain Stanley S. Nicolay, who shot down three Bettys during his tour with VMF-224, also commented on the problems of simply engaging the enemy.

"There were a lot of people out there who didn't get any (kills), but they worked their tails off. Shooting down an airplane is 90 percent luck; you're lucky if you find one. Most of the time, you can't. That sky gets bigger and bigger the higher you go.

"We had no radar. Even our radios weren't very good. We depended on our sight. Look, look, look, with our heads on a swivel."

USMC Aces During the Period August 1942-April 1944
* Awarded the Medal of Honor.

VMF-112:

Lieutenant Colonel Paul J. Fontana. 5 victories. Retired as a major general.
Major Archie G. Donahue. 14 victories.
Major Robert B. Fraser. 6 victories.
Captain Jefferson J. DeBlanc*. 9 victories (1 in F4Us).
Captain James G. Percy. 6 victories (1 in F4Us).
First Lieutenant John B. Maas, Jr. 5.5 victories.

VMF-121:

Lieutenant Colonel Donald K. Yost. 8 victories (2 in F4Us).
Lieutenant Colonel Leonard K. Davis. 5 victories.
Major Joseph H. Reinburg. 7 victories.
Major Francis E. Pierce, Jr. 6 victories.
Major Perry L. Shuman. 6 victories in F4Us.
Captain Joseph J. Foss*. 26 victories.
   Retired as a brigadier general in Air National Guard
Captain Thomas H. Mann, Jr. 9 victories.
   Also flew with VMF-224.
Captain Ernest A. Powell. 5 victories.
Captain Robert M. Baker. 5 victories.
Captain Donald C. Owen. 5 victories.
Captain Kenneth M. Ford. 5 victories in F4Us.
First Lieutenant William P. Marontate. 13 victories.
First Lieutenant William B. Freeman. 6 victories.
First Lieutenant Roger A. Haberman. 6.5 victories.
Captain Gregory K. Loesch. 8.5 victories.
Second Lieutenant Cecil J. Doyle. 5 victories.
Second Lieutenant Joseph L. Narr. 7 victories.

VMF-124:

Captain Kenneth A. Walsh*. 21 victories in F4Us.

VMF-212:

Lieutenant Colonel Harold W. Bauer*. 10 victories
Major Frank C. Drury. 6 victories (1 in F4Us).
   Also flew with VMF-223.
Major Robert F. Stout. 6 victories. Flew with VMF-224.
Captain Jack E. Conger. 10 victories.
Captain Phillip C. DeLong. 11-1/6 victories in
   World War II, two victories in Korea (all in F4Us).
Major Hugh M. Elwood. 5.1 victories.
   Retired as a lieutenant general.
Captain Loren D. Everton. 10 victories.
   Also flew with VMF-223.
Warrant Officer Henry B. Hamilton. 7 victories.
   Also flew with VMF-223.
Major Frederick R. Payne, Jr. 5.5 victories.
   Also flew with VMF-223.

VMF-213 (all kills in F4Us):

Lieutenant Colonel Gregory J. Weissenberger.
   5 victories.
Major James N. Cupp. 12 victories
Captain Sheldon O. Hall. 6 victories.
Captain John L Morgan, Jr. 8.5 victories.
Captain Edward O. Shaw. 14.5 victories.
Captain Wilbur J. Thomas. 18.5 victories.

VMF-214 (all kills in F4Us):

Major Gregory Boyington*. 28 official victories.
Captain William N. Case. 8 victories.
Captain Arthur R. Conant. 6 victories.
Captain Donald H. Fisher. 6 victories.
Captain John F. Bolt, Jr. 6 victories in World War II,
   six victories in Korea.
Captain Christopher L. Magee. 9 victories.
Captain Robert W. McClurg. 7 victories.
Captain Paul A. Mullen. 6.5 victories.
Captain Edwin L. Olander. 5 victories.
First Lieutenant Alvin J. Jensen. 7 victories.

VMF-215 (all kills in F4Us):

Captain Donald N. Aldrich. 20 victories.
Captain Harold L. Spears. 15 victories.
First Lieutenant Robert M. Hanson*. 25 victories.

VMF-221:

Lieutenant Colonel Nathan T. Post, Jr. 8 victories.
Captain Harold E. Segal. 12 victories.
Captain William N. Snider. 11.5 victories.
Captain James E. Swett*. 15.5 victories (7 in F4Fs)
Captain Albert E. Hacking., Jr. 5 victories (in F4Fs).

VMF-222 (all in F4Us):

Major Donald H. Sapp (later changed to Stapp).
   10 victories.

VMF-223:

Major John L. Smith*. 19 victories.
Major Hyde Phillips. 5 victories.
Captain Marion E. Carl. 18.5 victories (2 in F4Us).
   Retired as a major general.
Captain Kenneth D. Frazier. 13.5 victories (1 in F4Us).
Captain Fred E. Gutt. 8 victories.
Captain Orvin H. Ramlo. 5 victories.
First Lieutenant Charles Kendrick. 5 victories.
First Lieutenant Eugene A. Trowbridge. 6 victories.
Second Lieutenant Zenneth A. Pond. 6 victories.

VMF-224:

Lieutenant Colonel John F. Dobbin. 7.5 victories
Major Robert E. Galer*. 14 victories.
   Retired as a brigadier general.
Major Charles M. Kunz. 8 victories.
Captain George L. Hollowell. 8 victories.
First Lieutenant Jack Pittman, Jr. 5 victories.

VMF-321 (all in F4Us):

Major Edmund F. Overend. 8.5 victories, including
   5 with the Flying Tigers (3.5 in F4Us).
Captain Robert B. See. 5 victories.

TED WILSON

Henderson Field—Night.

Sources

Sources for this booklet fall into two basic categories: general historical publications for the overall situation in the Pacific, and references that describe specific subjects, such as aircraft, personalities, and campaigns. I found several general official and commercial publications invaluable, including LtCol Frank R. Hough, Maj Verle J. Ludwig, and Henry I. Shaw, Jr., *Pearl Harbor to Guadalcanal* and Henry I. Shaw, Jr. and Maj Douglas T. Kane, *Reduction of Rabaul*, volumes 1 and 2, *History of U.S. Marine Corps Operations in World War II*, (Washington: Historical Branch, G-3 Division, Headquarters, USMC, 1958 and 1963, respectively), and Robert Sherrod, *History of Marine Corps Aviation in World War II* (Novato, California: Presidio Press, 1980). Other general histories included, Peter B. Mersky, *U.S. Marine Corps Aviation, 1912-Present* (Baltimore: Nautical & Aviation Publishing Company of America, 1983, 1986), Masatake Okimuya and Jiro Horikoshi, *Zero!* (New York: Ballantine Books, 1956), and John Lundstrom, *The First Team: Pacific Naval Air Combat from Pearl Harbor to Midway* (Annapolis: U.S. Naval Institute, 1984).

Acknowledgements

The author would like to thank Maj-Gen John P. Condon, USMC (Ret), a fighter pilot and Cactus operations officer in early 1943, for reviewing the manuscript and making thoughtful and valuable insights. Gratitude is also extended to Dan Crawford, Benis M. Frank, and Regina Strother of the Marine Corps Historical Center; Dale Connelly and Rutha Dicks of the National Archives Still Picture Branch; and Robert Mikesh, James Lansdale, Henry Sakaida, James Farmer, and Linda Cullen and Mary Beth Straight of the U.S. Naval Institute.

About the Author

Peter B. Mersky is a graduate of the Rhode Island School of Design with a baccalaureate degree in illustration. He was commissioned through the Navy's Aviation Officer Candidate School in May 1968. Following active duty, he remained in the Naval Reserve and served two tours as an air intelligence officer with Light Photographic Squadron 306, one of the Navy's last F-8 Crusader squadrons.

He is the assistant editor of *Approach*, the Navy's aviation safety magazine, published by the Naval Safety Center in Norfolk, Virginia. Commander Mersky has written or coauthored several books on Navy and Marine Corps aviation, including *The Naval Air War in Vietnam* (with Norman Polmar), *U.S. Marine Corps Aviation, 1912–Present*, *Vought F-8 Crusader*, and *A History of Marine Fighter Attack Squadron 321*. He has written many magazine articles for American and British publications, and he also writes a regular book review column for *Naval Aviation News*.

WORLD WAR II

THIS PAMPHLET HISTORY, one in a series devoted to U.S. Marines in the World War II era, is published for the education and training of Marines by the History and Museums Division, Headquarters, U.S. Marine Corps, Washington, D.C., as a part of the U.S. Department of Defense observance of the 50th anniversary of victory in that war.

Printing costs for this pamphlet have been defrayed in part by the Defense Department World War II Commemoration Committee. Editorial costs of preparing this pamphlet have been defrayed in part by a bequest from the estate of Emilie H. Watts, in memory of her late husband, Thomas M. Watts, who served as a Marine and was the recipient of a Purple Heart.

WORLD WAR II COMMEMORATIVE SERIES

DIRECTOR OF MARINE CORPS HISTORY AND MUSEUMS
Brigadier General Edwin H. Simmons, USMC (Ret)

GENERAL EDITOR,
WORLD WAR II COMMEMORATIVE SERIES
Benis M. Frank

CARTOGRAPHIC CONSULTANT
George C. MacGillivray

EDITING AND DESIGN SECTION, HISTORY AND MUSEUMS DIVISION
Robert E. Struder, Senior Editor; W. Stephen Hill, Visual Information
Specialist; Catherine A. Kerns, Composition Services Technician

Marine Corps Historical Center
Building 58, Washington Navy Yard
Washington, D.C. 20374-0580
1993
PCN 190 003122 00

Made in the USA
Coppell, TX
27 June 2021

58166135R00026